Quite a Humdinger

The Life and Times of Captain George Thomas Worsham

An Autobiography
with help from Mike Schoeffel

"To reach a port we must set sail –
Sail, not tie at anchor
Sail, not drift."

- Franklin Delano Roosevelt

*This book is dedicated to
Jack Marshall, Margaret, Martha
my parents, Albert and Pansy
my brothers, Derwood and Hugh Ray
my kids, Tom, Vicky, and Sara
and my grandchildren.*

Contents

Foreword(s)...i

Preface...ii

Note about the Merchant Marines...vi

Author's Note...viii

Just a Good Ol' Boy from Kentucky...2

A Merchant Marine is Born...10

A First Thing Out of Hell...14

A Second Thing Out of Hell...18

Brothers in Arms...26

Rising Through the Ranks...30

The Hellraiser from Yugoslavia...41

George Ashore (Temporarily)...48

Regaining Sea Legs...52

Drunken Cooks and Rowdy Crews...63

George's Final Voyage – Battling Hurricane Josephine...67

Margaret's Trips...71

George Ashore (Permanently)...76

Losses and Gains...82

Bringing it All Back Home...89

Afterword...92

Foreword(s)

This memoir is much more than a personal history of my father – it captures the history of 20th century America. From the Great Depression, to the events of World War II, to Post-War America, my father's life represents the lives of ordinary people who did extraordinary things. These life stories represent what made America. What is truly extraordinary is they were done by my father. I love you, dad.

- Thomas Worsham, son

While I was growing up, Dad was gone a lot. It was his job, but as a child, I didn't understand. I just knew my Daddy wasn't home with us. I didn't understand what he did or what he went through to do his job. It was only as an adult that I started understanding. Listening to his sea stories sounded like books I had read. Finally, I started asking questions and more questions, and along with my brother and sister, we began to understand.

This is his story.

- Vicky Worsham, daughter

I have many great memories of my dad over the years, but probably the most special to me is when we got to meet him on his ships. If you've ever tried to get on a ship from a dock, you know there's a gangplank. I have been on a cruise ship before, but their gangplanks are nothing like the ones used for tankers. The rails are usually chains or rope, and there are openings between the steps that you could look through to see the water. I just knew I was going to fall through. I can remember standing on the docks, crying and refusing to go up. Members of the crew would try to bribe me with candy bars or money to get me to climb up, but I would just cry and say "I want my daddy."

When a ship gets to port, the captain is usually very busy, but my dad would always come and carry me up. So, you see, he has always been a hero to me.

- Sara "Jackie" Atkinson, daughter

Preface

"It's in our nature not to live long, and it's also in our nature to be a pair. That's the way the pattern goes. It's how we reproduce, renew the population of the Earth. We die off and new ones come on. It's a cycle." - Captain George Thomas Worsham

George is a part of the Greatest Generation, as it's often called, and as time continues to shove us headlong into the future, it becomes increasingly important that members of that generation preserve their stories on paper for future truth seekers to discover. As the march of time thunders forward, stopping for no one, each subsequent generation becomes further removed from the particulars of the lives of those who existed before them. Rural Kentucky during the Great Depression? World War II? Josip Tito's communist Yugoslavian regime? How can we, as outsiders to the Greatest Generation, come to truly *know* about these things?

Lacking direct contact with these places and events, they become nothing more than ideas to us outsiders, movies that play in our heads, a series of half-fictitious-half-real images entirely informed by films we've seen or documentaries we've watched or books we've read or stories we've heard. With a vibrant imagination, one can assemble a semi-real construct of what it was like to be alive during, say, World War II, a time when insanity on a global scale resulted in 50 to 80 million souls being vanquished from existence within a six year span. But that construct will never be anything more than a replica, because all of the images we possess are based on experiences other than our own.

To George, however, and many others in his generation, these events are authentic and tangible. The procession of images that plays in George's mind when he ruminates on that particular time period is based, first and foremost, on personal experience. That's an incredibly powerful perspective, and one that can help us create more accurate replicas to pass on to others. It's a first-hand viewpoint that fewer and fewer people possess with each thunderous stomp in Time's relentless march: Within the next 10-20 years, most members of the Greatest Generation will permanently check out, leaving countless valuable stories untold.

Thankfully, George's story will not be among these Lost Tales. In the twilight of his life, acutely aware of his finiteness ("It's getting close to the end of the line, I know that," he said recently), he chose to open up about his experiences so that others may understand what it was like to Be There at That Point in Time – and in turn, begin to build replicas to pass on to the next generation. The result of

George's willingness to reveal his unique viewpoint – especially his harrowing experiences at sea early in his Merchant Marines career – was a success on many levels.

During his 90th birthday celebration at his Hopkinsville, Kentucky home, surrounded by a gregarious gathering of friends and family, George finished recording his long and winding story on an old black tape recorder. The audio was converted into multiple MP3 files and sent to a transcriber, who turned George's somewhat muffled musings into over 40 pages (Calibri, 11-point font, in Microsoft Word) of material. After the transcription process was complete, I began receiving the transcriptions – piecemeal, in Word documents via email – from George's oldest daughter, Vicky Worsham. Thus began the process of turning these formless (but intriguing!) chunks of text into a coherent narrative that told George's story as clearly and accurately as possible. It was around the end of November 2014.

I won't bore you with the mundane details of how the thing finally came together (hint: a lot of caffeine, many hours in front of a computer screen, and several borderline psychological breakdowns), but I will say it was one of the hardest and most rewarding undertakings of my life. Fortunately, George knows how to tell a good story – in that dry-humored, Kentucky gentleman, no frills type-of-way – and that made it a lot easier to mold his words into, first and foremost, something that he and his family can pass down through the ages, and secondly, a biographical work that folks outside George's intimates may be able to enjoy on a pure entertainment level.

While that second distinction would be a welcomed byproduct of commercial publication, it certainly isn't the ultimate aim of this book. I don't know if anyone other than George's tight-knit crew will read these pages. To me, that's okay. If, in 2115, or another year in the not-so-distant future, George's great-great-grandchild takes this book off the shelf, dusts it off, and learns something new about his/her family – his/her *heritage* – then all of the recording, transcribing, editing, proofreading, arranging, writing, reediting (x1000), and publishing will, I think, be fully validated for everyone involved.

***

This is Captain George Thomas Worsham's story. After you read it, pass it on.

Keep his voice, and the voices of others from the Greatest Generation, alive in the face of that pounding, continuous drumbeat.

- Mike Schoeffel

A Note about the Merchant Marines

It's true that the Merchant Marines are not an official branch of the military, but as you'll come see within these pages, the line between "military" and "non-military" was dog-hair thin during WWII, if not non-existent all together. German U-boats, it seems, did not disseminate between "combat" and "non-combat" Allied ships. During a time of heightened paranoia on a global scale, lines in the sand were dangerously black and white: to a German U-boat captain, an Allied ship was the Enemy, even if it didn't have militaristic capabilities. Seamen aboard Merchant Marines' ships were often thrown into situations just as precarious as their military brethren, if not *more* precarious, considering they carried no weapons and were often aboard ships loaded with barrels of oil and/or fuel. George's recollections in chapters three and four of this book are prime examples of just how dangerous life could be for a Merchant Marine between the years of 1939-45.

The fact that it took the U.S. Government over 40 years to grant WWII Merchant Marines veteran status is not only a puzzling injustice to those seamen who suffered through horrific scenes of cataclysmic death and grave injury, but also seemingly a marginalization of the startling Merchant Marine death toll in WWII. During those six harrowing years, one in 26 Merchant Marines perished[1]. Compare that ratio to the Marines (one in 34) and the Army (one in 48) and the dangers Merchant Marines faced during the greatest military conflict in human history become painfully and undeniably clear.

The experiences printed on the following pages are pulled entirely from George's absorptive mind. While some of the details may have become inadvertently twisted by the wringing passage of time, the emotional thrust of George's experiences remain intact.

Nothing has been purposely fabricated.

---

[1] According to statistics compiled by Captain Arthur R. Moore in his work *A Careless Word - A Needless Sinking: A History of the Staggering Losses Suffered by the U.S. Merchant Marine, both in Ships and Personnel, during World War II.*

Editor's Note

This book has been written in semi-linear fashion. Some of the chapters progress sequentially through George's life, while others don't contribute to the forward momentum of the narrative. The reasoning behind this structural choice has to do with the fact that the dates for some of the stories were tricky to pin down, yet either too important to George's life, or too entertaining, to omit entirely.

To read this book in chronological fashion, skip chapters 5, 7, 10, and 12.

GTW

Part One

1
Just a Good Ol' Boy from Kentucky

"Someone told me once, 'It's time to get you a pair of overalls, boy.' But I don't believe in summing up nothin' – I let my experiences speak for themselves." – M.C. Humphreys

"Everyone in our town has a story..." – Carsten Jensten

I think I am beginning my book. It's hard to start, but I think I'll begin at my birthday.

My name is George Thomas Worsham, and I was born on May 2, 1924 in Christian County, Kentucky. My parents were Albert and Pansy Worsham. At the time of my birth, they were living on E 7th Street in what they now call the Old West House, which is on the Historical House, recorded in history – not from my birth, but from someone else's. My parents were farm people, born and raised. My pop was working as an electrician at Ball Electric, and my mom was a homemaker that took good care of me. My maternal grandfather, Ark Dickerson, was working on a big plantation in South Christian called the Cherry Farm, and he invited mom and pop to live there and help out. So that's what they decided to do for a couple years.

Eventually, my parents decided they wanted to go out on their own, so they became sharecroppers on the Berry Farm close to Pilot Rock. There was a plain old dirt road in front of the farm called Pilot Rock Road, and it was seven miles from the end of it to Hopkinsville. The grocery store was two miles from where we lived. Pop furnished all his own tools and was working on commission, receiving 2/3 of the profit while the landlord, Mr. Berry, got 1/3. It wasn't a bad deal.

My memories begin on the Berry Farm when I was 3 or 4 years old. My parents had about eight acres of dark tobacco, which was a bit of a chore to set, to say the least. One spring, I came up with a debilitating arthritis-like ailment and couldn't walk for a while, so they put me on a sled and pulled me behind a mule to the tobacco field. Mom worked in the field, just like pop, and I played on the sled while they set tobacco. That was the thing of it: back then, *everybody* worked. There wasn't much time for play.

Mom raised chickens for eggs and had three or four milk cows, too. She made butter and had some loyal customers in Hopkinsville. Every Saturday, we would load up the horse and buggy and "clop, clop, clop" nine miles into town to sell products to her regulars. East 7th street was blacktop, and the old horse would keep "clop, clop, clopping" as we breezed down the road. At that time, there were far more horses and buggies than cars. We would deliver her stuff and she would get cash. In the summertime, we would take 100 pounds of ice back to our ice box.

※

By the time I turned six I had to enroll at Laytonsville School, which was about two miles from the Berry Farm. There were no school buses, so we had no choice but to walk. I gathered with a few kids that lived close to me and we strolled together every morning, messing around the whole way there. Milton Shaw (who was about 18 years old at the time) and I were the only boys in the school, and there were about 10 girls. Needless to say, we had our pick of the ladies. We started school in July, and in October, a bad cold spell rolled through that forced us to build a fire in the wood burning stove at the school house. It was the first time a fire had ever been built at Laytonsville, and wouldn't you know it, the entire school burnt to the ground. It took a couple of months to rebuild, and during that time I didn't have to go to class. Sounds nice, but they added the time on at the end of the year. We didn't' get out for Christmas, either.

When I was about 7 or 8, we moved from the Berry Farm to a place closer in town called Fruit Place. It was a sharecropping deal just like the Berry Farm. By the time I was 9, I started bugging my pop: "Let me plow! Let me plow!"

One day he said: "OK, we're going to give it a try. You can plow that watermelon patch this afternoon."

The mule he gave me was hard of hearing. I would say "Whoa!" but he would just keep right on going. I always kept two lines on him that I would pull back on when I wanted him to stop. Letting my pop know I could plow turned out to be a big mistake, because after that there was no excuse for getting out of plowing. I began my compulsory work with corn, plowing it with a coulter[2] before it was ready to harvest. Boy, I must have walked 10 miles up and down those corn rows. In the early autumn, we plowed the biggest part of land we planned on working with the following spring. We had a single turning plow to do all of this. It had wings on the side, and it turned the dirt over as you and two mules pulled it along. When spring came, we got ready to plant the corn. We'd cut off the sassafras bushes, stack 'em, then burn 'em.

---

[2] A coulter is a three-bladed plow with two handles that is pulled by a mule as you walk behind it.

By that time, pop was working full-time in Hopkinsville at a meatpacking place called Pennyroyal Packing Company. While he was gone, I was the main humdinger when it came to operating the farm. The plow I used was pretty efficient, but what I really wanted was a Ford tractor like our neighbor, Jim Williamson. It was the only one in the entire neighborhood. It had these enormous steel wheels and was used mostly for breaking and disking the ground. Pop made a deal with Jim that allowed us to use the tractor to get the cornfield up. Jim had a son who would drive the tractor while I rode along. It didn't take me long to figure out how to do it properly, and once I did, Jim's son and I had an absolute ball.

I did my fair share of misdeeds during childhood, with perhaps the worst being the time I broke my father's plow to get out of a day's work. I figured if I broke the point on the plow and took the mules to the stable, I could free up the rest of my afternoon. That sounded pretty good to me because I wanted some play time, so I turned the plow on its side and broke off the point with a grubbing hoe.

That was the worst thing I could have done. Pop was making about $12 per week and commuting seven miles per day to Hopkinsville for work. So we were by no means rich. I didn't tell pop about my misbehavior until after I retired from the Merchant Marines many years later. I had bought a farm down in Trigg County, Kentucky and pop was living with us. One day, I mustered the courage to admit the truth.

"Say pop," I asked him. "You know how the point got broken on that turning plow?"

"Well, no," he said.

That's when I told him. He was upset, but not overly so. It had been bearing on my mind for many years, and I was glad to have it off my chest.

※

Throughout my childhood, it always seemed like we were on the move. My parents eventually made a deal on another farm up at Bootstrap called Cushman Place, which was right behind a church we attended. It was a very old house, and I slept upstairs next to a window. All of our heat came from a wood burning stove, which meant I had to cut a lot of wood. Mom also cooked on that stove.

Sometimes the heat wouldn't reach my sleeping area very well. The snow blew in through cracks in the window and often when I woke there was a layer of white fluff on top of my quilt. I would lie in bed as long as I could, then bolt downstairs to the fireplace. That's where we took our clothes off and got dressed.

We ate well, no doubt about that. Mom and pop were skilled farmers. Cushman Place had a nice garden and a brooder house for the chickens, and one of my jobs was to fire the furnace to keep the chickens warm. Mom raised a couple hundred chickens, and they would huddle around that thing, shoulder-to-shoulder, trying to increase body heat. By the time they were two-to-three pounds they were primed for market. My mom made a little money in that.

I changed schools when we moved to Cushman Place. But my parents wanted me to finish up the year at Laytonsville before I transferred, so they boarded me on a nearby farm and paid for me to stay there. The family I lived with had a son who was about 20-years old. He loved to hunt for coon, possum, and rabbit. I learned a lot from him, and we got into a little mischief, too.

I was still in grade school when I finished at Laytonsville. That next fall, I enrolled at Ralston School: a one-room school house with a single teacher who taught all the grades. About 30 kids went there. A bunch of us joined up every morning and walked the road together, similar to when I lived on Berry Farm. I met my first sweetheart, Virginia Jones, at Ralston School. I was deeply in love. I also loved baseball, and we played a lot of it at Ralston. Every Sunday it seemed like we were somewhere playing a ball game, and I ended up becoming a pretty talented catcher. We had some red hot games, no doubt about that.

One interesting thing about Ralston School is that we didn't have running water. Outside, there was a big country hole with a seat on top, and that's where we crapped. There was one for the boys, one for the girls, and they were quite a ways apart. We got our water from a big sinkhole with a stream running through it about ½ mile from school. It didn't take long for us to realize that volunteering to go to the spring was a great way to get out of class. Some people made home brew and kept watermelons down there. I didn't bother much with the home brew, but I sure did like those watermelons.

When pop went to Hopkinsville for work, we had to get the car out: a '28 Chevy straight shift. The first time I got behind the wheel, it was stuck in mud almost up to the axel. To pull the thing out, pop fetched the mules and tied them to the front bumper. I can still see it: I was in the driver's seat mashing the pedals, but boy, it was as stuck as could be. I shifted into low gear, but forgot to release the clutch. Pop was yelling "What's wrong? The back wheels aren't turning!" The mules were pulling as hard as they could and I was revving the engine like a madman with the clutch jammed all the way to the floor – it was a hell of a scene. Finally, pop noticed what I was doing wrong and shouted: "You have to let off the clutch!" We eventually got it out. Pop didn't give me too much grief about that, though he easily could have. I guess you can say that's how I learned to drive a five speed.

After I graduated eighth grade at Ralston School, my family moved to Hopkinsville because the long haul to work was getting pretty rough on pop. In the fall of 1939, I started high school in Hopkinsville, which was located about four miles from our house. I got a new bicycle so I could swiftly cover the distance. My two younger brothers, Derwood and Hugh Ray, were going to Perry School at the time. They were about nine years younger than me, and starting to get up there in years.

*
**

Pop had to be at work at six in the morning, so he would drop me off at school on his way through. We had to leave the house extremely early every day, and it was my job to make sure all the cows were milked before we began our journey. In the afternoons, I got out of school around three and pop worked until about five, so I spent those extra three hours practicing with the football team.

By the time senior year rolled around, I was getting pretty sick of school. Skipping became my new favorite pastime. When pop found out about that, he gave me an ultimatum. He said: "Son, you either have to go to school or go to work." By then, I had fallen too far behind to go back to my studies. So I chose work. I was about 16 when I dropped out, would have been 17 when I graduated. Pop had connections at the grocery store and hooked me up with a full time job. I got paid eight dollars per week plus room and board. They had a store room with a bed, and that was my domain for a while.

I had a lot of fun at the grocery store, starting out as a delivery boy and working my way up the ladder. I will never forget the old delivery van that I drove: it had mechanical brakes that I had to mash on to make them work. I had a few close calls, but no wrecks. I eventually graduated from the delivery van to the meat counter, where I held the title of main butcher's apprentice. We sold a lot of stew and hamburger meat to grocery stores, eventually gaining enough popularity to receive standing orders. I worked as an apprentice for about a year and ended up getting pretty skilled at it. I cut the heck out of my right hand, but that's just part of the job. You can always tell a butcher by his scars.

I quickly found out that work was not a very good thing to get into. By the time I came to that realization, a war was on, the greatest military conflict in human history, and I would find myself out at sea before my 20th birthday.

2
A Merchant Marine is Born

"There is one rule, above all others, for being a man. Whatever comes, face it on your feet."- Robert Jordan

On April 1, 1943, when I was 19 years old, I started my three months training with the Merchant Marines. I decided to become a Merchant Marine for a number of reasons: First of all, one of my friends had joined a few years prior, and he had returned to Hopkinsville on vacation with a thick stack of 100 dollar bills. That interested me. Secondly, I knew a draft was approaching, and I wanted to control my own destiny, not have it determined by the powers that be.

The Merchant Marines are responsible for transporting cargo and passengers, and during wartime, can be called upon as an auxiliary to the Navy. Although the Merchant Marines aren't technically a branch of the military and don't officially have a role in combat, I didn't know any of that when I joined. I thought I would have the opportunity to shoot guns and battle the Axis Powers. Even though that's not how it panned out, I would come to find out that just because I wasn't technically in the military didn't mean I wasn't going to encounter wartime conditions.

At the time, Merchant Marines' training was patterned after Navy boot camp. There were about 30 other guys with me in Division 36. I was a dishwasher in the galley for about a week- pots and pans were my thing - before my superiors said "That old boy needs to go up a little further." They put me on the Joseph Conrad: a three-masted square rig schooner used for training. I was in unknown territory at that point, but I followed orders to the "T" and everything worked out. We learned how to tie knots and splice and other useful tricks – seamanship is what we were aiming for.

Training on the Joseph Conrad was a memorable period of time for me. I had never been on a schooner in my life and the Conrad is a *big* schooner: 105 feet from the deck up to the cross arms on the main mast, which was where I was stationed. Whenever the ship set sail, I went up the rope ladder and climbed onto the top cross arm. There were three of us on each side of the mast, and we untied the lines from the sail to let it loose. Naturally, it picked up wind. That was our sign to come down the tight wire rope. We climbed down hand-over-hand, using our feet as brakes if we were moving too fast. It was an enlightening experience, and I felt like I was learning something.

I'd often go to bed beat tired. As soon as I thought I was going to get a good night's sleep, they'd issue an emergency fire and boat drill. One night, we rode a lifeboat around the ship from midnight until four in the morning. There were at least 30 of us in that lifeboat, and it was only about 30 feet long. To stay fresh, we changed ore people every so often: I'd row for a little bit, go down in the bottom of the boat to rest, and come up again to row. Around and around that ship we went. After a week on the Conrad they sent me back to base.

I had a six-week preliminary training course in St. Petersburg, Florida that started on April 6, 1943. I accomplished a lot there, furthering my legitimacy as a qualified seaman: rules, regulations, customs and traditions, VDIG selection and classification, physical training, marching, swimming, first aid, resuscitation, firefighting, boat rowing, sailing, rafting, beach buoy, gun, gas mask and gas chamber, life preservers, knots, and gunnery. That equaled out to 144 hours.

There are three departments in the Merchant Marines: the deck, the engine and the steward. I was sent to the deck, which meant another three months of specialized training in St. Petersburg. I logged 58 hours of Western conference lookout and standby, five hours of bridge and equipment, 36 hours of cargo hatch and cargo work, five hours of ship education, 10 hours of mast rigging, 10 hours of ground tackle, three hours of maintenance, 10 hours of modeling seamanship, 15 hours of preparation for the Able Body Seaman exam, 72 hours of deck seamanship, and 30 hours of general drills for a total of 254 hours.

For the first six weeks we were required to stay on base, but eventually we were granted shore leave in St. Petersburg. At the time, St. Pete was an old person's town, but there were a few happenin' hotspots, including this one bar not too far from base where we spent most of our time. We didn't go ashore much because we were only being paid about $36 per month, but every once and a while we'd go have some fun. One time, I came back to base from St. Petersburg a little too drunk and tried to fight three or four dudes. They put me under right away. Needless to say, I learned that picking fights was not a smart thing to do.

We spent most of our time sailing around Tampa Bay. For a 19-year old boy who hadn't seen much of the world, it was all new and exciting. In the past, for training, young Merchant Marines had sailed to Havana, Cuba, but that was out of the question for us due to the threat of German U-boats. After training, I spent two weeks at upgrade school in Lake Pontchartrain, New Orleans, learning how to sail a lifeboat. Every morning we piloted a lifeboat around the lake. We were allotted some liberty at night, which was nice, because there was a park not too far from the base that had rides and all sorts of attractions. *Our* main form of entertainment, however, was picking up the ladies.

Needless to say, I enjoyed myself there.

After Lake Pontchartrain, I was sent to Mobile, Alabama with two or three other guys to board a Liberty Ship[3]. There was all kind of random junk on there: Mostly war equipment, but a lot of miscellaneous stuff, too. When we got to Mobile, the older sailors frowned down on us because we were young seamen without much experience. But I was a confident son of a buck, and I held my own.

---

[3] A Liberty Ship is a ship filled with dry cargo

3
A First Thing Out of Hell

"Come away, O human child!
To the waters and the wild
With a faery, hand in hand
For the world's more full of weeping than you can
understand." – W.B. Yeats

The Liberty ship sailed from Mobile, and we joined a convoy of about 20 ships outside Mobile Harbor. The plan was to go around the coast of Florida and up to New York to pick up deck cargo. Everything was going neatly, but not long after we got around the tip of Florida, I got my first bitter taste of war.

I was in the bunk when the general quarters started wailing. I jumped up, forgetting to put on my shoes. I grabbed my life jacket and headed to my prearranged position at the forward gun tub, stumbling over a pad eye and hurting my foot along the way. That was one thing I learned: put on your shoes before you hit the deck.

When I reached the deck, it was in a state of chaos. German U-boats had been waiting to prey on our convoy as it came up the coast, and they attacked with speed and gusto. They got seven of our ships that night, one of which was a tanker close to my ship. It was undoubtedly loaded with aviation gasoline because it went up in a burst of flames when the torpedo penetrated its hull. Now in this world, it's hard to imagine, but I was close enough to the flaming ship to see people desperately trying to escape. As we passed, I saw about 15 guys in a pack on the catwalk. They would run to one end, see there was no way out, rush back toward the stern, only to find no outlet there, either. Our ship passed coldly on. I don't know what happened to those guys, but I'm sure all of them perished. The deck was in flames, the gasoline was burning on the water. There was no way out. It was a thing out of Hell, you know?

We made our way to New York City. The U-boats must have given up on us because the scene started to calm down. In the distance, I saw seven ships completely engulfed in flames. That made me think: "What the hell am I doing here?" We went back to our bunks, but our thoughts were much different than when we left there. We were hardly broken into wartime conditions; this was something most of us had never experienced. It wouldn't be the last time I had a near-death encounter with the Germans and their shadowy U-boats.

When we arrived in New York, they tied us up at a Brooklyn dock. Brooklyn felt like a foreign country to me. I couldn't understand anything the stevedores were saying, moving this way and that, shouting at one another and securing the deck cargo. They spoke a dialect totally lost on me. They loaded us up with airplanes, landing crafts, and other types of cargo. During the war, there was a mark on each ship called a "plimsoll mark." By law, it designated the deepest you could load the ship before it lost stability. The stevedores paid no attention to the "plimsoll mark" during the war – it wasn't unusual for it to be a couple feet underwater.

***

After we loaded the deck cargo, we went to anchorage and waited to form a 40-ship convoy headed to Halifax, Nova Scotia. Regulation called for 1500 feet between each ship, but stealth was of top priority, so no ship was allowed to use its lights. As one could imagine, this made it difficult to adhere to regulations. It takes some humdinging to keep a ship in line when everything is blacked out. My buddy Jack Marshall – who I'll talk about a lot later on – did it, but I never did.

When we got to Grand Banks, Newfoundland we ran into fog so opaque that we couldn't even see the ship in front of us. It was like being completely blind. One night, there was a submarine alert and they dispensed our convoy. Each ship was supposed to follow a course to minimize the chance of a collision. But not every ship followed that course, and we ended up in two wrecks in one night.

In the first incident, we kissed off the side of another ship and stuck our anchor in its side. The two ships kept drifting around each other until the captain on our ship gave full ahead. He figured we were dead meat for an enemy submarine if we kept sitting there in the water. We removed our anchor, but lost it. We hadn't gone much further when "BANG!" we plowed into an English ship at full speed. We were dead in the water for a while, trying to figure out what the hell to do next. Eventually, the English ship sunk. Years later, I received letters from people who had relatives on that ship wanting to know if I had any information about the incident. I didn't have much to tell them. All I knew is that we hit a ship and it had disappeared into the depths of the ocean.

So not only did we not have an anchor, our bow was all caved in, too. After a while, the convoy gathered and headed to Manchester, England by way of Liverpool. That in itself was an experience. The Manchester Canal is a beautiful thing. We discharged our cargo and sailed to Liverpool to get our bow mended before heading back to North America.

I was still only 19 years old at the time, exploring the sea and learning a lot about the world. Soon enough I would find myself face-to-face with death, asking myself, yet again, "What in the hell am I doing here?"

4
A Second Thing Out of Hell

"In the presence of the storm, thunderbolts, hurricane, rain, darkness, and the lions, which might be concealed but a few paces away, he felt disarmed and helpless."- Henryk Sienkiewicz

"His body tensed as his gut was struck with a frozen bullet of shock. He couldn't breathe."- Sidney Knight

We were five days out of England when we ran into a pack of German U-boats while I was on a four-day watch on the lookout. Out of nowhere, I saw the stern of the ship next to us violently rise up: a torpedo had struck it in the fourth and fifth cargo hole. That's when all hell broke loose.

A torpedo had hit us in the engine room. I felt a blast of air, but didn't hear any noise. That was the amazing thing: When you're close to an explosion, you're deaf to the noise, but you feel the air pressure rush past you. I was up in the gun tub when it hit, and it felt like I had been whacked in the face with a wooden plank. It knocked me flat on the floor, and while I was down there, desperately trying to regain my senses, a second blast hit me. At the time, I didn't know we were hit. I didn't know anything, for that matter. It was sheer confusion. I just knew my lifeboat station was on the starboard side. I had to get there.

The telephone was dead, so I crawled out of the gun tub and descended to the deck on an iron ladder. When I got to the number three hole, there was a crack across the deck about three feet wide, exposing the interior part of the ship. I leapt across the gap and ran to the lifeboat station. There stood a chief mate and two or three other people, horror etched on their faces. The lifeboats were secured over the side. The ship was breaking in two, right where I was standing on the stern.

A big wave was headed my direction. With my lifejacket secured, I grabbed onto the rail and held on for dear life. I thought the wave would come in, go back out, and everything would be fine. Instead, the water rushed over me and stayed there, submerging me for what felt like hours. That's when I turned to religion. I said a prayer: "Father, I am too young to die, please let me live," and let go of the railing. To this day, I don't believe I would have made it without some help from a higher power.

My life jacket brought me to the surface, right through a patch of Number 6 fuel oil. I was completely coated in it. In retrospect, the oil is probably why I'm still here today because it covered my exposed areas and kept hypothermia from setting in. After I wiped the oil from my eyes, I glanced up: The ship was gone. I grabbed onto a 3x6 hatch board that was floating on the water as debris surfaced all around me. A wooden boom that held the cargo on our ship kept coming up and going down right beside me. I said to myself "I have to get away from this, because it's going to come up directly underneath me."

I spotted two guys in a four-man life raft. They came over and let me on board. Eventually, we located the deck engineer from my ship and brought him on board, too. He was badly shaken, so the three of us took turns consoling him. Half the time we couldn't keep a life jacket on him. He was so mentally and physically beat up that he kept taking it off and tossing it to the side, like a useless piece of junk. There were other guys loose in the water, too, grabbing onto anything that would hold them. Some people were screaming in agony, others were shaken but uninjured, others still were moaning solemnly, slowing ceding to that slow black train of death.

We started moving away from the wreck, wary of the great suction that occurs when a sinking ship begins to fill with water. When we finally got relatively clear of the area, we came across another guy in the water. We couldn't let him on, of course, because we were already full-up, but we let him hold onto the raft for a few minutes. Eventually, he made his way aboard another life raft. He survived.

During this time, our naval escort was making passes through the area, throwing off depth charges[4]. I recalled what they told me in training at St. Petersburg: get your balls out of the water, because depth charges can cause you to go sterile. I think it was a load of bologna because it didn't affect me at all (I ended up having three kids, after all).

We managed to drift far away from the wreckage. There was one English rescue ship making the rounds, its sole purpose

---

[4] A depth charge is an explosion that goes down a certain distance and will sink a submarine if it hits it.

to pick up survivors. The sea was rough that morning, with 8-10 foot swells. When we reached the top of a swell we could see the ship, but when we went down in the valley it was nothing but water. We figured the rescuers would eventually spot us, but when we saw the rescue ship take up its lifeboat, we started to panic. I thought "Oh man, they're going to leave us here to die." We hollered and hollered, doing everything we could to get their attention.

Miraculously – at least to us – the rescue ship didn't desert us. The rescuers were just afraid they would lose their life boat because of the rough seas. We drifted for a while, and finally the rescue boat pulled up beside us and threw us a scramble net. Three of us climbed up as fast as we could, but the deck engineer couldn't manage it. I think he was already dead in the lifeboat, but they pulled him on board just to make sure.

We were still coated in oil when we got on the deck, so the rescue crew stripped us down. Once that was done, we were stark naked, confused, and freezing cold. They tossed our contaminated clothes over the side and wrapped us in a blanket. Then they sent us to the bunks and served us a cup of rum I quickly drank down. That's when the shivering started. If you've had a chill, you know it usually only lasts a short period of time. This chill, however, was resilient, refusing to subside. The rum warmed me up, but never completely took the chill away. I shook and shook and shook, eventually falling asleep. When I woke up, the only thing on my mind was "Who survived?"

We started talking amongst ourselves. Out of our whole convoy – about 35 ships – 12 merchant ships and three escorts were sunk. One of the escorts, a Canadian Destroyer called the St. Croix, had 147 people aboard. One person – W.A. Fisher from Alberta – survived. Of the 75 crew members on my ship, the Theodore Dwight Weld, 43 were never heard from again – lost at sea. Like I said, when I was holding onto that railing underwater I said "God, I am too young to die." I believe that's why I'm still here today. I beat the odds, somehow or another.

We were relieved to reach the rescue ship, but our troubles were far from over. For 10 days it was depth charge after depth charge, torpedo after torpedo – I heard them whizzing by the hull of our ship. The journey back to Halifax was very nip-tuck. We were sunk on Sep. 20, 1943 and reached shore on Oct. 1.

Once we got there, the injured were hospitalized and the healthy went to the Red Cross for baths. That was the first bath I had taken since I left England, and it felt great. The Red Cross gave me clothes and a goody bag that included a razor, a toothbrush, and other toiletries. We stayed there for three days before the War Administration made arrangements for us to go to New York City.

The only clothes I had were what the Red Cross gave me. All my papers – *everything*, really – had sunk with the ship. Once we arrived in New York they put us in a hotel and gave us our money. Oddly enough, they cut off our pay precisely on Sept. 20 – the day the ship went down. That didn't make any sense to me, considering we were still in grave danger for 10 days on the rescue ship.

I stayed in that hotel until I was fully recuperated. Coincidentally, a guy from my hometown, Hopkinsville, happened to be in New York City when the New York Times ran a photo of some of the survivors, myself included. After he learned where I was from, he called my parents to tell them he had met me and that I was OK.

The New York Times ran the story of our plight in the Oct. 2, 1943 edition of the paper, the lede of which goes like this:

A pack of U-boats believed to have used a new and deadlier type of torpedo, followed two Canada-bound convoys "like a school of sharks" for ten days last month and sank ten and possibly eleven Allied vessels, including three warships, surviving seamen disclosed today.

The enemy submarines, returning to the North Atlantic in apparently great numbers after several months of comparative inactivity, continued the attacks until the convoys were almost within sight of the Canadian coast line.

And then, six paragraphs later:

Survivors of two American and one Norwegian cargo ships gave a word picture of one of the starkest sea fights since the war began. They told of ships breaking in half as torpedoes ripped into their hulls, of injured and dying men struggling for hours in the icy, oil-thick water on the outer rim of the Arctic circle, of exploding depth charges and of one U-boat being blasted out of the water after being caught in the beam of a warship's searchlight.

I caught a train and left New York, heading home to Kentucky for a 30-day leave, a much different man than when I left there.

Part Two

5
Brothers in Arms

"Be near your brothers. Not just one, but both of them."-
Fyodor Dostoyevsky

I have two brothers: Derwood, who was born in 1932, and Hugh Ray, who came to Earth 18 months later. There are eight years between Derwood and I. As we went through life, I was always gone – out at sea and what have you – and Derwood looked up to me as a good friend. He joined the Air Force after World War II and served 21 years before retiring. He had a very distinguished service, working as air police in Vietnam and earning a silver star.

He also spent some time as an Air Force police officer. One morning, on his way to work, he received a call on his radio describing two suspects in a bank robbery. Lo and behold, the car these two criminals were in drove up directly in front of him. He phoned in for back-up and ended up nabbing these two bank robbers. Old Derwood was a hero, there's no doubt in my mind. And it wouldn't be the last time he came through in the line of duty.

Derwood was gung-ho in everything he did, and he quickly climbed the ranks in the Air Force, making it all the way to security chief. After he retired from the military, he met a girl in Spokane, Washington, and they got married and had three kids. He was a golf fan all his life, and I always enjoyed visiting him because Spokane has 18 golf courses and our goal, until he passed away, was to play them all.

After military life, he became an assistant security chief at Spokane International Airport. During his time there, a 24-

year old man by the name of Larry J. Bonner walked into the airport with a rifle, taking an airport worker hostage and demanding a plane. In the heat of the moment, Derwood shot the potential highjacker, saving God knows how many lives. He received the Federal Aviation Administration's Distinguished Service Medal for his heroic actions.

Here's how the April 5, 1982 edition of the Spokesman-Review described the incident:

"I saw him coming around the corner [outside the terminal] on two wheels," remembers Lee Holford, the airport's operations director. "I was going to go out and say something to him. It's a good thing I didn't."

What Holford and the other authorities didn't know was that 24-year old Larry J. Bonner had just killed his wife with a shotgun at their Chesney, Wash., home – and he wanted to get out of town, fast. Bonner, armed with a rifle, shot an Air Force sergeant outside the terminal door in what Worsham says was an attempt to create a diversion.

Bonner then walked up to the ticket counter and grabbed a National Weather Service electronics technician as a hostage. He was beating the man with the rifle, screaming "Gimme a plane! Gimme a plane!" when Worsham appeared on the balcony above.

"I'm always in the wrong place at the right time," Worsham said with a chuckle. "[Bonner] slapped the hostage back against the ticket counter. That gave me room to shoot."

Worsham shot, and hit Bonner square in the face.

"I've never seen anybody shook up so bad as that young guy from the weather bureau," Worsham recalls. "Of course, I shot within 18 inches of him."

And after he did, Holford points out, Worsham ran right over and administered life-saving techniques to Bonner, who was sent to prison on murder and assault charges.

For his part, Worsham was awarded the Federal Aviation Administration's Distinguished Service Medal.

Eventually, Derwood's wife passed away, and not much later Derwood died, too. He had diabetes that he never took care of and it finally caught up with him. Derwood lost one of his sons, Jimmy, but his other two kids are still alive. I communicate with them every so often. Not as much as I should, but you know how it goes.

***

My other brother is Hugh Ray. He's trying to get as old as me, but he's never going to catch me. Hugh Ray was in the Navy for four years, but left the military after one enlistment to pursue a career in computers. He landed a job in Chicago, working as a technician on this giant computer. It was about 50 feet long and five or six feet wide, and it took 21 technicians to operate it. And to think - nowadays we have these tiny phones that can do more than that huge computer could ever have thought about doing.

Hugh Ray eventually became a salesperson for a telephone company that gained popularity during the computer boon. He has three kids, just like Derwood did. All of them graduated college and ended up with good jobs in Seattle. When Hugh Ray retired, his wife, Marilyn, followed suit, and they relocated to Seattle to live close to their grandkids. They reside in Maple Valley, just outside Seattle.

Hugh Ray is 81 years old now. His birthday is May 3 and mine is May 2. Spring babies. He has this blind poodle that he takes down to the coffee shop every morning. The dog doesn't drink coffee, but Ray Hugh does. A lot of it.

6
Rising Through the Ranks

"Act the way you'd like to be and soon you'll be the way you'd like to act."- Bob Dylan

Two months after I nearly lost my life off the coast of England, I got job as able bodied seaman on a ship named the Oscar Chapel. On our first journey, we met up with a convoy of about 40 ships along the East Coast, headed for England, traveling at about eight knots.

The convoy split: some of the ships went into the Irish Sea, Liverpool, and Manchester. Others, like mine, headed to London. We were in convoys of 12 off the coast of Lockhue, Scotland, when we abruptly changed course. The ship on the inside of us slammed into our starboard side, opening a hole 14-feet wide and 28-feet deep. The other ship backed out, but by that time we were sinking. Thankfully, we were close to a beach and in no grave danger. We ran aground and discovered that over 100 plates had been damaged in the bottom of the ship.

We waited in Scotland for about a month while a salvage boat made repairs. During that time, water mixed in with the fuel oil and caused an explosion in one of the boilers so violent that we thought we had been bombed. Tug boats pulled us to a dry dock in Liverpool, and we stayed there for three months while repairs were made.

We had day work from 8 a.m. to 5 p.m., but after that, seamen with money to spend were allowed to go ashore. Our favorite place was a hotspot for Merchant Marines called the Ocean Club. There were a lot of black American soldiers there at the time, and they employed some pretty interesting pick-up lines on white British women. I remember this group of colored guys, on several occasions, telling women that the American Army had inoculated them with a substance that turned their skin black. I'm not sure if that one ever worked for them, but damn if it wasn't creative.

Liverpool had been heavily bombed by the Germans early in the war, and the streets were scattered with rubble. It was a pitiful sight to see. There had been no attempt to rebuild, and the city was completely blacked out – no street lights, no lights shining out of windows, nothing. I had a chance to talk to several British citizens during my time there, and I gained a lot of admiration for them. They are a tough, determined people, even when their beloved city was in ruins.

This was right before the June Allied invasion of Normandy, so England was swollen with American GIs. Everybody knew something big was about to go down, the only question was "What?" In May, the Oscar Chapel was ready to sail. One month later, the Allies launched Operation Overload against the Nazis on Omaha Beach, the biggest singular invasion in human history.

We made two quick trips to Halifax carrying ammo before heading back to the states. Thankfully, the North Atlantic had cooled down by then and there were very few German U-boats in the water. I got off the Oscar Chapel on June 1, 1944 and headed home for 30 days. On June 30, I went to

Houston to join the T.E. Mitchell, another Liberty ship. We loaded ammo, drums of aviation gasoline, and numerous airplanes, and departed to Bombay, India. Our journey took us through Gibraltar, the Mediterranean, the Suez Canal, the Red Sea, and the Indian Ocean. India was a real eye-opener for me: I thought I was poor growing up as a sharecropper in Kentucky, but my humble lifestyle was nothing compared to lowly Bombay.

***

After discharge, we went to Portugal, which was neutral at the time and a trading place for prisoners of war between Germany and the Allies. There were a lot of Germans roaming around, which made us all a little anxious, but we didn't experience any conflict. Eventually, we gathered a load of coal and headed to Santos, Brazil. In late November, we unloaded the coal and started loading 200-pound bags of coffee. We shipped the parked cargo to an offshore island called Angra dos Reis, which, in English, means "Island of the Kings." When we were finished, the girls in Santos were very happy to see us.

On my final trip with the T.E. Mitchell, we delivered 10,000 tons of coffee beans to the Maxwell House coffee plant in Jacksonville, Florida. I got off the T.E. Mitchell on January 4, 1945, and a month later I signed on as a deckhand on the Phoenix, the largest tanker in the world. Time was moving fast, and I was experiencing a lot of new and exciting things.

We loaded 30,000 tons of aviation gasoline and departed for a port near London. The Phoenix was a fast ship, but the ocean is No Man's Land no matter how rapidly you're moving. I couldn't help but think back to those horrible scenes I had witnessed as a young Merchant Marine. It gave me pause. Thankfully, we didn't run into any U-boats that time around.

At the time, the Nazis were sending buzz bombs toward London, and I can still remember the first time I heard one: It sounded as though a plane had flown overhead and cut off. A few minutes later, a big explosion occurred in the direction of London. I knew what that meant.

***

In England, March of 1945, I met a fellow seaman by the name of Jack Marshall. Jack would become a lifelong friend. I will never forget the morning our paths crossed for the first time. I was a deck mate, and the able bodied seaman who was supposed to be on watch came down with an illness, so they put me on watch with Jack. Things can get rather lonely up there, and around 2 o'clock in the morning Jack finally broke the silence.

"Where you from?" he asked.

"Hopkinsville," I said. "Hopkinsville, Kentucky."

It turned out that ol' Jack was from Clarksville, Tennessee, which is about 30 miles south of Hopkinsville. Our high schools routinely played one another in football, and it was always a rough game. They eventually had to discontinue the rivalry because a free for all fight broke out after one particularly violent contest.

Soon after we met, Jack and I headed to Baltimore to study at Moore's School of Navigation. Jack was going for his Second Mate license and I was aiming to become a Third Mate.

The test went way over my head. I learned some geometry and trigonometry in high school, but a lot of water had passed under my bridge since then. Thankfully I had a dedicated teacher, and Jack kept the pressure on. Finally, my time came for the exam. I went to Custom House in Baltimore, entering at 8 a.m. with nothing but a pencil in hand. I approached the inspector's desk and he gave me a card filled with questions. There was a time limit, so I couldn't screw around, and I didn't have an adding machine, either. I began on Monday, and by Friday I had passed with a brand new Third Mate license, which meant I could ship out as an officer. Jack passed his exam, too, and we celebrated as friends and shipmates.

It felt good to be an officer, it meant I was making progress.

***

On August 29, 1945, I was assigned to my second tanker: the Nashbulk. The war was ending in Europe, but still humming along in the Pacific. Our first destination was Pearl Harbor, and we docked near Battleship Texas, which was just returning from a tour in the Pacific. It was amusing to watch the crew go ashore dressed in pristine whites only to come back a few hours later drunk and disheveled.

Captain Henry Ziskowski was in charge of the Nashbulk. He was a good skipper, and he took it upon himself to make a quality mate out of me. At first, I could do nothing right, and he gave me hell every time I made a mistake. I was young, dumb, and didn't have much love for him at the time, but I later came to appreciate how he helped me become a well-rounded mate. He was a tough dude, almost like a father figure, in a sense, considering I was still very much a young man.

Captain Ziskowski was a real character. He brought this little dog on a lot our trips and that thing would yip and yip, like a buffoon. One time, when we reached port, a few seamen and I were discharging cargo when all of a sudden that mutt came bounding down the gangplank and onto the dock, yipping all the way. It was our job to watch the cargo at all costs, but we couldn't just sit there while the Captain's dog split for God Knows Where. So we stopped what we were doing to track down this son of a buck. The dog thought we were playing with him, he was having a grand old time. Eventually, we corralled him, and everything turned out alright.

Now Captain Ziskowski was married, but he wasn't the most loyal husband in the world. He lived in New England when he wasn't out at sea, but he had a girlfriend down in Texas that would join us on the ship every so often. She slept in the Captain's quarters with ol' Ziskowski. One day, while I was on watch at a port, he grabbed me by the shoulder and pulled me aside.

"If my wife tries to board the ship, don't you dare let her on," he snarled.

"OK," I said. "No problem."

Sure enough, a few minutes later, that dang woman came marching toward the ship. She must have smelled something amiss. I was nervous as hell as I stepped in front of her and threw up my hand.

"Ma'am, you can't come aboard right now," I said. "Doesn't matter who you are."

She was having none of it.

"Like hell I can't!" she shouted, pushing me aside and striding up the gangplank.

A few minutes later, I heard a hell of a racket coming from the Captain's quarters. I said to myself, "Whoa, boy." I figured that Ziskowski was going to eat me alive, and that my job was finished. Surprisingly, he never said much about it. Eventually, Ziskowski and his wife got divorced, and that was pretty much the end of it.

Life wasn't smooth all the time, that's a fact.

***

Jack and I got off the Nashbulk in February of 1946. About a month later, the National Bulk Carriers put us on a tanker, which was smaller and slower than the Nashbulk. The captain – Captain Jim – was a laid back 69-year old who basically let Jack run the ship on his own. Jack had earned his Chief Mate license, so that's the rank he assumed. When the ship was sent to Mobile for repair, every member of the crew was laid off except Captain Jim, Jack and I. That was an enlightening glimpse into the fickle nature of seafaring life.

During the rest of our time on the tanker, Jack and I split the watch: he was on for 24 hours, I was on for 24 hours. It worked out well. Around this time, I decided it was time to keep moving up the ranks. So I went to work for my Second Mate license. It was a hard exam, and I had to do more studying than I had ever done before, but I passed. Captain Jim was full of pride when he awarded me the promotion. I beamed with confidence.

As time passed, National Bulk Carriers wanted Jack and me to join another tanker together. The only trouble was I would have to sail under the Panamanian flag. Normally, that wouldn't be allowed, but Panama offered a license equal to that of an American license. After some deliberation, Jack and I decided accept the offer. We set sail in June 1947 with more than 30,000 tons on board.

There was a machine shop down in the heart of the ship that Captain Bird used to make these little toy trains. He constructed the wheels, the axles, the whole thing, and had a miniature railroad system snaking all around his office. It was an amazing sight to see. Our crew was a rough and diverse group from Skid Row in New York. Thirteen different nationalities were on board, and the boatswain, a Romanian, could speak five different languages. He was our big communicator when we reached a foreign port, considering ol' Jack and I couldn't even speak English all that well.

We didn't have much trouble at sea, but those Skid Row boys could get extremely rowdy at port. Jack and I would often have to pacify the situation. There was one Spanish clique of about eight guys that stuck together like brothers. I was on watch one night, waiting to be relieved at midnight. But when the clock struck 12, the seaman that was supposed to relieve me - a big Cuban who ran with the Spanish clique - didn't show up. I trudged down to the bunks, searching for this son of a buck.

I found him sprawled out in his bed, passed out from heavy drinking. I shook him vigorously, but he didn't wake up, so I slapped him across the face. Nothing. Determined to get this guy out of bed, I filled up a bucket of ice cold water and tossed it in his face. That got him. He flailed his arms and started hollering like a madman. I told him to get his butt up to the watch right away. Thinking he would follow me up in a few minutes, I left him to regain his senses.

A few minutes passed and he still hadn't shown up. Around that time, I heard a ruckus coming from the captain's quarters in the midship house. I hurried down to see what the heck was going on, and all of sudden the Cuban came running out, ol' Jack on his tail, booting him in the behind with this pair of farming shoes he always wore. It was the damndest sight. When the scene calmed down, I pulled Jack aside.

"What in the world *happened*?" I asked.

"That son of a bitch came at me with a *knife!*" he said. "I was lying on the couch, taking a nice little nap, and woke up to this Cuban hollerin' and screamin' with a knife right in my face!"

By this time, the Cuban had scurried off again, so Jack and I set out to track him down, once and for all. We found him mingling with that Spanish clique of his. We nabbed him, chunked him in the paint locker, and shut off all the lights. It was completely dark in there, almost like sensory deprivation. We kept him isolated for a while to expedite the "sobering up" process.

***

As time moved on, Jack married a girl named Charlotte. Soon thereafter, I met him in Baltimore and we went back to the Moore's School for more test taking. Jack was going for his Master's license and I was going for my Chief Mate license. I passed my exam, but Jack, being newly married, hadn't studied much. He failed the first time he took it, but passed a month later.

After I received my Chief Mate license, Jack and I spent about seven years on different ships. National Bulk Carriers put me on a T2 called the Evans Creek for a quick trip to the Persian Gulf. By then, most of the captains I interacted with didn't give me a hard time because I was well-versed and competent. After my time on the Evans Creek, I went home to Kentucky to find my parents renting a place on Old Madisonville Road in Hopkinsville. I had a good bundle of cash saved up, so I put a down payment on a house on 19th street. That was one of the best things I've ever done. It was their home for the rest of my mother's life.

Eventually, I made my way onto another T2, the Callabee. We were at sea for about 10 months, and when we got back in March of 1951, I returned to Moore's School in Baltimore to work on my Master's License. More studying, another test. That was the hardest exam I had taken up to that point, it covered all three territories of the ship – the deck, the engine, and the steward – because a Master needs to be ready to deal with all situations on any part of the ship. I passed on May 5th, 1951. I was thoroughly satisfied because it had been a major goal of mine.

I went back to Kentucky to celebrate. Meanwhile, National Bulk Carriers was downsizing. They had started with 51 ships under the American flag and were down to three. The rest of their ships had been moved to Liberia and Panama. Jobs were becoming scarce, so I took that as a sign that it was time to put my seafaring career on hold for a while. I framed my Master's License and looked at it every now and again.

Old West House on East 7th street in Christian County, Kentucky, my birthplace and home until the age of three.

I attended Ralston School, a one-room school house, while I lived on the Berry Farm with my parents. Some of my fondest childhood memories were formed here: I met my first love, Virginia Jones, played a lot of baseball, and ate watermelon that was kept in a stream about 1/2 mile behind the building.

My parents, Albert and Pansy Worsham, one month after their wedding. They are dressed in the same clothes they wore to the ceremony.

Me at the age of five

My brother, Derwood, and I hanging out on top of a horse. Derwood was in born 1932, eight years after me. He went on to serve in the Air Force for 21 years, earning a Silver Star in the Vietnam War. He also served as assistant security chief at Spokane International Airport for many years.

Derwood, Hugh Ray, and I playing pick-up football in our backyard.

My father, two brothers, and I in 1942, about a year before I officially joined the Merchant Marines. I was 18 years old.

All dressed up in the spring of 1943, just a few weeks before I left for Merchant Marine training in St. Petersburg, Florida. I was 19 years old.

Dressed up in my Merchant Marines uniform shortly after joining the service in 1943. I was 19 years old when this picture was taken.

Me (far left, seated) in Halifax, Nova Scotia less than a month after the Liberty Ship I was on, the Theodore Dwight Weld, was sunk by torpedoes from German U-boats. The other seamen in the picture are (from left, seated) James MacNeil, Campbell Scott, Dann Gregg, and William Duffy. This photo appeared in the Oct. 2, 1943 edition of the New York Times.

Me, as a shirtless third mate, scrubbing away at the bold-face NASHBULK sign, circa 1945.

One of my best friends, Jack Marshall, mends his sailing apparel while smoking a pipe. I met Jack on the U.S.S. Phoenix in 1945, and soon thereafter became close, lifelong friends. We sailed together for the better part of 17 years on various ships before he retired from the Merchant Marines in 1967.

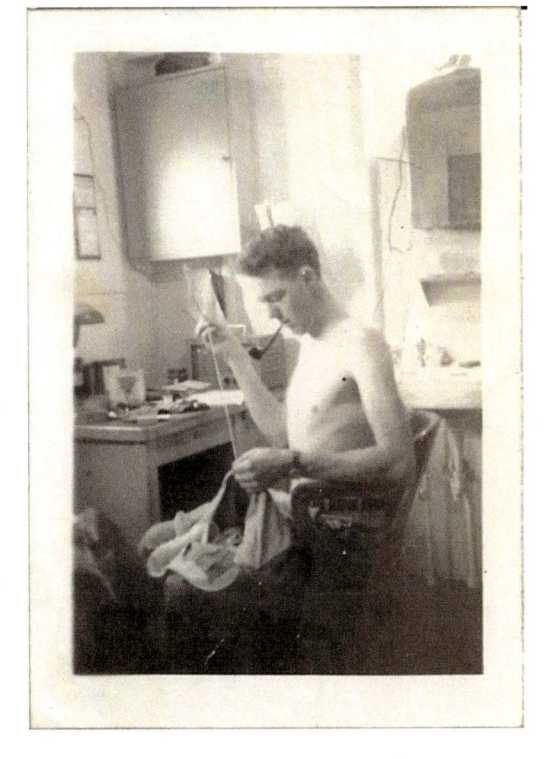

The Rock Cafe on North Main Street in Hopkinsville as it looked when the "Three Musketeers" - Denton Foster, Jimmy Garr, and I - owned it during the 1950s. My family and I lived on the second story of the building for the better part of a decade

The house on 19th street in Hopkinsville that I helped my parents buy around 1950. They lived there until my mother passed away in 1988.

Margaret and I share a kiss on our 50th wedding anniversary in Pigeon Forge, Tennessee.

Margaret and I fooling around with Rosie the dog at our house in Powhatan, Virginia.

The Joseph Conrad, the ship I used for Merchant Marine training. It was in St. Petersburg, Florida when I trained on it, but has since moved to the Mystic Seaport, in Connecticut.

The whole Worsham crew in Powhatan, four days after Christmas in 1998. From left, me; Caitlin Worsham, Tom and Terry's daughter, my granddaughter; Terry Worsham, Tom's wife, my daughter-in-law; Jacob Atkinson, Jackie and Harry's youngest son, my grandson; Harry Atkinson (d), my son-in-law, Jackie's husband, Tom's best friend; Tom Worsham, my only son; Sara (or Jackie) Atkinson, my youngest daughter; Matthew Atkinson, Jackie and Harry's oldest son; Margaret Worsham, my wife (d); and Vicky Worsham, my oldest daughter. Not pictured: Meghan Worsham, Tom and Terry's daughter, my granddaughter.

Martha and I were married at Rocky Ridge Church in Trigg County on January 29, 2004.

My old friend Jack Marshall attended my 90th birthday celebration at my home on 2002 Lover's Lane in Kentucky.

The crew at my 90th birthday party in Kentucky. From left, Vicky Worsham, my oldest daughter; Sara (or Jackie) Atkinson, my youngest daughter; me; Meghan Worsham, Tom and Terry's daughter, my granddaughter; Tom Worsham, my son; Caitlin Worsham, Tom and Terry's daughter, my granddaughter; Martha Worsham, my wife; Terry Worsham, Tom's wife, my daughter-in-law.

My son, Tom, and I standing in the bleachers at the old Hopkinsville High School football stadium in January 2015.

My grandson, Josh Purdum, and his family paid a visit to my Kentucky home in April 2015. From left, top row, me; Martha, my wife; Josh Purdum, my grandson. Middle row, Kameryn Purdum, my great granddaughter; Gabi Purdum, my great granddaughter. Bottom row, Leila Purdum, my great granddaughter; Olivia Purdum, my great granddaughter.

My whole family got together for a cookout in Powhatan on a fine spring day in April 2015. From left, top row, Sara (or Jackie) Atkinson, my youngest daughter; Varna Boyd, Margaret's niece; Matthew Atkinson, Sara's oldest son, my grandson; Meghan Worsham, Tom's oldest daughter, my granddaughter; Leila Purdum, Josh's daughter, my granddaughter; Josh Purdum, my grandson; Caitlin Worsham, Tom's youngest daughter, my granddaughter; Tom Worsham, my son; Vicky Worsham, my oldest daughter; me; Martha Worsham, my wife. Bottom row, Kameryn Purdum, Josh's daughter, my granddaughter; Olivia Purdum, Josh's daughter, my granddaughter; Bucklee, Tom and Terry's dog.

My grandson, Jacob Atkinson, and I at Capital Ale House in Midlothian, Virginia in April 2015.

7
The Hellraiser from Yugoslavia

"The Edge: there is no honest way to explain it because the only people who know where it is are the ones who have gone over." - Hunter S. Thompson

Gino was a good friend of mine with an interesting history, and I'm going to recount some of it here. His dad owned Marine Carriers, a steam ship company that, at one time, possessed about 15 ships. His dad was a non-U.S. citizen in New York when the U.S. entered WWII, and the American government gave him the option to remain in the country if he turned over one of his ships to the Allies. By and by, he was granted citizenship. As an aside, Jack Marshall and I ended up working for Gino's dad and Marine Carriers for several years. On the company's final ship, the Producer, I was named Senior Captain, an incredible honor.

Gino was born in communist Yugoslavia during Josip Tito's oppressive regime. If it was found out that a citizen was dissenting against the government in any way, even speaking out against it, that person could be thrown in jail and have his commodities cut off. In 1949, I experienced, first-hand, how bad things were in Gino's home land. We arrived on a ship carrying Number 6 oil during a time when the U.S. was trying to create good relations with Tito. We were basically trying to win him over by feeding him oil. The Yugoslavian people were in terrible shape. I couldn't believe the uncomfortable quality of life there. It was poorer than poor: serf-like. Worse than Bombay, even.

We were granted shore leave, but no one took it. There was nothing there to look at, nothing to do. It was endlessly bleak. The only time we could talk to anybody was when we were unloading cargo, and everyone I met told a sad tale. I wish anybody who has dreams of socialism could have heard their stories, because they were never optimistic. We left Yugoslavia later in the year, and I didn't go back until Tito was gone and the government had changed philosophies.

Gino fled the country during Tito's terrible reign by stealing a small boat and rowing it across the Adriatic Sea to Italy, where he received political asylum. That put him on Tito's Death List, but Gino is sly, and Tito was never able to hunt him down. Gino ended up in New York, working as an agent for his father at Marine Carriers.

Gino was a good friend, but he would make some of the damndest deals you've ever seen. On one particular trip to Pakistan, he got there a few days before the ship arrived and made shady arrangements. He was a fixer, and he often set up sketchy plans and saddled the captain - in this case, me - with the responsibility of making sure everything unfolded smoothly.

In Pakistan, it was possible to hire workers to perform maintenance - such as derusting and repainting the ballast tanks- for far cheaper than in the U.S. The Captain (me) always had a certain amount of American money for these jobs. When we entered port in Pakistan, we went through custom house and declared our American money. The official exchange rate was three rupees (the currency in Pakistan) to one American dollar, but on the Black Market, it was nine rupees to one American dollar. So Gino convinced me to change out my dollars on the Black Market and pay off these workers to help with the ship. I met some people who agreed to give me 45,000 rupees for $5,000. That sounded good to me, so I hopped into a taxi cab with a group of shadowy dudes.

We were supposed to drive around the block and come right back, but it didn't happen that way. We puttered around for at least 30 minutes, and I grew concerned when we entered a dangerous part of Karachi. We pulled up to this farmer's market, where we exited the cab, walked across the street – past colorful produce and dangling meats – and entered another cab on the other side. They must have thought the secret police was after us, because after that we drove around aimlessly for another 30 minutes. Finally, we pulled into the parking lot of the largest bank in the city, where this guy slinked out the back door. I gave him my American dollars, he gave me my rupees, and we took off in the taxi.

We retraced the route we had taken there: back to the market, into another cab, and on to the American Consulate. I did business and cleared the ship for the next port. There were customs guards at the gate, and I didn't know for sure whether they had been paid off. I had all these freaking rupees, so I sweated it out until I reached the other side. Once there, I breathed a deep sigh of relief.

I climbed back on the Producer, safe and sound, and said "Man, I will never do that trick again!" I swore it off. Gino tried to persuade me to take part in his sketchy plans a few more times, but I flatly refused. That's the sort of stuff Gino used to get me into, and that's life in the Middle East, too – don't believe anything anybody tells you. They're out for your money over there, and life is very cheap.

*
**

Another time, before the rupees incident, Gino purchased this ship that had been used as a United States spy ship for several years. It was docked in Mobile, Alabama, and Gino needed a use for it, so he called me up and asked if I was interested in making some extra money.

"I'm always interested in a little extra money," I told him.

He said he had a contract to ship bananas with a company in Colombia. The lone catch was the entire eight-person crew was from Honduras, and only one of them spoke English. It was a shoestring operation, to be sure, but I agreed to it, thinking it might be fun: I would bring my wife with me, and we could take a vacation or two for free. But as I've learned many different times during my life, ideas don't always match up with reality. Working on that damn banana boat caused more gray hairs than any job I've ever done. I've never worked so hard in my life.

On our maiden voyage to Colombia, we sailed past Cuba on the east side, making sure to stay 15 miles off shore. Had we sailed any closer, we would have been in Cuban territory, making us free game for Cuban gunboats. I never laid eyes on a gunboat, but I knew they existed.

We sailed past Cuba, eventually hitting tradewinds from the East that caused angry, 10-foot swells. It was getting pretty rough on deck: we were bouncing around and carrying on, and at 3 a.m. the power completely shut off. I'm talking no lights, nothing. I was asleep at the time, but one of the crew members woke me up and broke the harrowing news.

"We're out of fuel," said the one shipmate who spoke English.

That's a desolate feeling, thinking you're stranded in the middle of the Caribbean with no gas.

Now it's kind of hard to explain if you're not familiar with the anatomy of a ship, but there is a thing called the "settling tank" and another thing called the "double bottoms." Normally, oil is suctioned up into the settling tank from the double bottoms, but on this particular occasion the suction was negated by the rough seas caused by those tricky tradewinds. So, we weren't technically *out of oil*, the turbulence had merely stalled this process and kept oil from making it into the settling tank.

The crew and I went below the deck, armed with flashlights and several five gallon buckets. We formed an assembly line, of sorts, between the double bottoms and the settling tank, filling up the buckets with oil and passing them, person-to-person, up to the settling tank, where they were dumped. We repeated that process until enough fuel had been transferred to reach port. Eventually, the generator cut on, negating the necessity of flashlights and removing some of the drama from our prickly predicament.

We got the ship in working condition and finished out the trip to Colombia. But thanks to our temporary, unintentional pit stop in the middle of the Caribbean, we arrived a day late. Normally, this wouldn't have been a big deal, but when it comes to shipping bananas, things can get tricky. They have to be exported while they are still *very* green, because it takes a while to get them across the water, and once they arrived back in Tampa – which is where we were taking them at the time – they still had to be loaded onto trucks and hauled to Nashville, Louisville, or St. Louis. It's a long process, and once one bushel of bananas starts ripening, it releases CO_2, causing all of the bananas around it to begin the ripening process, too. Before you know it, you're stuck with a ship full of over-ripe bananas nobody wants.

Well, the Colombian company had jumped the gun on cutting the bananas from the tree, figuring there was no way we would arrive late. When we pulled into port, there was a train loaded with bananas about a quarter mile long slithering its way through the Colombian countryside. The inspector turned down every last piece of produce. He was right to do so, because there was no way they were going to make it back to the states without rotting. All of the bananas were dumped, and we took the blame. We waited there for three or four days while the Colombian company hacked another order of yellow fruit from the trees.

During that time, I received a telegram from the company back in the U.S. telling me to give them a call. They instructed me not to use a phone owned by the Colombian company, which meant I had to go to the local telephone operator. Back then, you couldn't just pick up a phone and make a call. I waited at that place for dang near six hours. When I finally touched base with the company in the states, they told me they had a hunch that the Colombian company was using the bananas as a ruse for importing narcotics. I'd bet my last dollar they were right. I had the same feeling.

After the three day wait was over, and the bananas loaded, we headed back through the Caribbean to Tampa. When we got there, customs agents did a quick sweep of the cargo. It was a pretty slack search and they didn't turn up anything illegal. All in all, I did that banana trip to Colombia five times. When we arrived in Tampa on my second trip, there were about 50 customs officials waiting for us. They had picked up the scent of a possible drug smuggling operation. They tore through every last box, desperately trying to turn up *something* illegal. But they never did. We were clean, at least on that trip.

That was the only time in all my trips to Colombia that we were searched intensively by customs officials. On the other trips, the search was a mere formality. I never found any drugs amongst the bananas, but then again I never looked all that hard. I suppose I'll never know if I inadvertently brought narcotics across our borders.

8
George Ashore (Temporarily)

*"Recreate your life, always, always.
Remove the stones, plant rose bushes and make sweets.*

Begin again." – Cora Coralina

Back on land for an extended period of time for the first time in almost a decade, I decided to head back to Kentucky to pursue a more traditional way of life. I had two buddies living in Hopkinsville named Jimmy Golf and Denton Foster. Everyone called us the Three Musketeers. Denton was a good promoter, and he came up with the proposition of starting a restaurant together. We discussed buying a place on North Main Street called the Rock Café. I was the only one of the Musketeers with money at the time, so I financed it. I didn't know crap about running a restaurant, and neither did Denton, but we decided to take a chance. The first thing I did was hire a bookkeeper, that's the one thing I did right.

We got our menu down. Our clientele was mainly business people. We sold a businessman lunch for 75 cents that came with meat, three vegetables, a drink, and a dessert. As you can imagine, we had to sell a hell of a lot of business lunches to cover $1200 a month in overhead. If you don't think it's tough coming up with $1200 in nickels and dimes, try going through it yourself.

The bookkeeper kept us on the straight and narrow. He let us know when we weren't calculating our food percentages correctly. We sold the popular beer brands like, Oertel's 92, for 15 cents a bottle. Premium beer, like Schlitz and Budweiser, was 20 cents a bottle. Coffee was a nickel per cup. We had to keep the customers flowing to make any semblance of a profit.

After about six months in business, I noticed money vanishing from the cash register. I came to the conclusion that Denton was to blame, so we promptly split partnerships. Though married with kids, Denton had been having a fling with one of the waitresses. I also think he was having financial issues at home, which gave him motivation to steal from the restaurant. After he left, management was short-staffed, so I really had to buckle down.

Not long after we opened the restaurant, my life changed in a major way. A girl named Margaret Boyd was staying with her mother, Florence, at a motel near the Rock Café. She and her mother came into the restaurant several times, and on one occasion, she parallel parked on the street. As they were leaving, Margaret's mother opened the driver's door and a car sped past and knocked the thing off. Naturally, they had to stay in town a few extra days while the car was being repaired. During that brief window, Margaret and I ended up getting friendly together. She was 23 and looking for a husband and I was 27 and looking for a wife. We met on June 1, 1951 and on July 4 we were married. If it wasn't for that incident with the door, I probably never would have met her. It's right strange, when I think about it. After we tied the knot, we moved into an apartment located on the second floor of the Rock Café.

We stayed together until she passed away in 2003. Our first born, Thomas, showed up on April 17, 1952. Not too long after that, Vicky was born. Then, in 1957, Jackie came along. After Jackie's birth, I joked with Margaret, telling her "We have to stop this." I'm proud of my kids. They're good people and they've done well for themselves.

***

We were putting in a lot of hours at the restaurant and had the wild trio running around at home. Life was a big bowl of cherries. But, as I would come to find out, the restaurant business can be very confining. We often opened at 6 a.m. and didn't close until midnight. Around 1955, I grew weary of the long hours and started getting involved in trucking with Lonnie Gamble, hauling rock and asphalt for a stone company. I installed fertilizer spreader beds in two trucks, and got a job spreading bulk fertilizer with the Virginia Carolina Fertilizer Company.

As I made my foray into the trucking business, Margaret spent a lot of time operating the restaurant. Running two businesses eventually got to be too much, so we sold the Rock Café to a guy named MacIntosh who was expanding a restaurant he had in Hopkinsville. He kept it for about a year before selling it to another guy, who ended up running it for almost 30 years. It's still a restaurant today, still on North Main Street, although the name has been shortened to "The Rock."

Not long after becoming involved in the trucking business, I tried my hand in produce. Lonnie helped with that, too. He was a real enterpriser. I knew a lot about ships, but nothing about produce, so Lonnie showed me the ropes. We fixed up a fruit stand in the early part of May 1958 and started hauling watermelons out of Florida. We retailed them at a few locations around town, and the grocery stores in Hopkinsville were buying them wholesale. We had a routine route, selling watermelons to grocery stores in several little cities, including Madisonville and a few others.

Margaret and her mother, Florence, helped out immensely while I was immersed in trucking and produce. Florence did her fair share of babysitting. In the fall, the guy who owned the land we were renting wanted it back, so we had to relocate. We found a place on North Main Street to lease and fixed up a fruit market, a produce market, and sold Sinclair gas. We used the Sinclair service station to buy gas for our trucks wholesale.

I stayed in the trucking and produce business for a while, but came to decide I was working only for the bank and the insurance company. Margaret was working her butt off, I was working my butt off, but at the end of the year, we didn't have much money to show for it. Plus, the bug to return to the water was hitting me harder than ever. I had kept my Master's License up to date, so one day I told Margaret "I'm ready to go back to sea."

The pull of the open water was too great to resist.

9
Regaining Sea Legs

*"My soul is full of longing
for the secret of the sea,
and the heart of the great ocean
sends a thrilling pulse through me." - Henry Wadsworth
Longfellow*

Around 1961, I called Jack Marshall to see if he could hook me up with a job. He said "I'll see what I can do." Not long after I talked to him, I received a phone call about being a Chief Mate on a T2 tanker called the Almena. I said "Yes sir, I'm ready!" They told me to join them in New York.

It had been a decade since I had set foot on a ship and I was concerned I had fallen behind the times. A guy at the union hall told me "Man, I wouldn't take you back, not even as a *Third* Mate. You've been 10 years ashore, and you expect to come back and be a *Chief* Mate?"

I told him, "We'll see how it goes."

When I walked on the Almena, it was like stepping back in time. The ship was laid out exactly like the last ship I had been on, the Callabee. The captain was an American, but of Yugoslavian descent, so he didn't speak very good English. Still, we hit it off pretty quickly. We left the states, and I was gone from home for 17 months. I got a chance to see Margaret a few times when she visited at different ports.

The Almena was an old ship. It was built during WWII, and we received limited permission to sail with cargo out of Portland, Oregon. After that, the Almena was supposed to go to the Breakers – a graveyard for ships, essentially – but it didn't pan out that way.

We left our port heading toward Japan, and not too long after departure we encountered a tremendous storm. I'm talking 70-foot waves, some of the biggest I've seen. The Almena was on its last legs, but we surged forward. We burned a lot of extra fuel fighting those waves and barely made it to Hakodate, Japan intact. After reaching Hakodate, we went to India for a load of grain oil, thinking it would be our last assignment. But lo and behold, we got cargo out of the Persian Gulf and set sail for Marseille, France. And when we got to France, we had a charter with NATO, which had fuel scattered in different places in the Mediterranean for us to pick up. We set out for about six months to retrieve it all. It was a real humdinger. We brought it all to the NATO fueling station in Palermo, Italy and finished up the charter. The Almena held up just fine.

From Palermo, we went to the Persian Gulf and picked up a load of Number 6 oil for the Navy and headed toward Okinawa in Buckner Bay. We had some difficulties unloading because of the age of our ship – some of the pipelines had holes and we had to patch them up because they were forcing air into the pumps. Our pumps couldn't push enough oil up to the booster pumps that were positioned 300 feet up a mountainside, so the thing kept shutting off. We had a hard time, but eventually finished the job.

From Buckner Bay, our orders were to go to Taiwan to take the Almena to Breakers, good old ship that it was. We arrived at the south end of Taiwan in a town called Kaohsiung. They weren't quite ready for us to deliver her to the breaking yard, so we anchored outside the port with no shore leave, patiently awaiting orders. To pass the time, I watched Chinese fishermen attempting to catch these 20-30 foot long spotted sharks. The fishermen were using relatively small boats, and they'd bait the shark into coming to the surface and stick it with a harpoon. The shark would take off and pull the boat around and around at high speeds. It was quality entertainment.

Eventually we sailed inside and they tied the Almena at the dock. When we pulled in, they were breaking down another ship. I'm still not sure how they did this, but they began cutting it apart at the top, and whittled it down until there was only a small portion left floating in the water. The Chinese are very intelligent; they don't spend money if they don't need to. Another thing I noticed is that at least 1/3 of the people working in the yard were women, and none of them were overweight. They were all slim and trim and I can understand why: their diet is mostly rice and they work exceedingly hard.

Once we got inside the breaking yard, they tied up the Almena and took me and the 39 crew members off. They had chartered a DC3 plane to carry us from Kaohsiung to Taipei. It was a very old plane, and when they closed us in you could see daylight shining in around the door. Quite unsettling. It had a capacity of 39 people, and that's exactly what we flew. We landed on an old dirt runway, and ended up staying in a hotel for five days until we departed for Tokyo. The hotel catered more to Western-style food and it didn't cost us a cent because the company was covering everything. It was an enjoyable stay.

I was really impressed with the Chinese way of life. There was a park across the street from the hotel, and every morning it was filled with people exercising. The plane finally arrived to take us to Tokyo, where we stayed overnight. I bought my wife a set of authentic pearl necklaces. Jackie ended up with those pearls, and she wore them at her wedding. They put us on a plane to San Francisco the following morning.

I don't know if you've ever ridden on a plane with a bunch of seamen, but they tend to get rowdy. We were coming home after a hell of a long stay over in the East and the flight attendants were *really* free with the booze. You can imagine what happened. The pilot almost turned the plane from San Francisco to Alaska to dump some of these guys off because they were starting to get out of control. I was in first class, and the crew was in tourist class, so the attendants – who were getting more anxious by the second – wanted me to quiet them down. Little did they know, you can't quiet down a drunken seaman. They're going to do what they want, and if you try to stop them, they won't hesitate to fight you. We finally made it to San Francisco, without too much incident. After that, I took a much-needed 30-day vacation.

*
**

In 1967, Jack decided to call it a career. He had spent 20 years in the Merchant Marines, and he felt like it was time to move on to other things. I joined Jack for his last trip at sea: a three month journey to India. That was the first time we had been together in almost a decade, so we had a lot to talk about. Nothing particularly exciting happened during those three months – no storms or aggressively drunken cooks or anything like that – but it was nice to spend time with Jack before he packed it in.

When he told me of his retirement to me, tears welled up in the corner of his eyes. I think it broke him up a bit, considering how long he'd spent at sea. But Jack is a self made man with many passions, and he has flourished in retirement. When he was at sea, he constantly read farming magazines, and right before he retired, he bought a 300-plus acre farm in Clarksville for $19,000. He farmed to his heart's content until he got so old he couldn't farm any more. Cattle were his thing. To this day we are good friends and I try to see him as often as possible.

*
**

Around this time, I bought a little cabin cruiser named the Daydream from a company called Bambi's Cruisers. During World War II, it had been used as a patrol boat in the Chesapeake Bay, and it was coated in this ugly grey paint called "Wartime Grey." When I bought it, I replaced it with beautiful mahogany and slick oak framing.

I owned it for about four years, and during that time a man died on it.

I was heading out to sea – where to I can't quite remember – and before I departed I hired this guy to put a coat of barnacle paint on the bottom of the cruiser. At one point, the boat had been patched underneath with low-quality caulking, so while this guy, Mr. Williams, was applying paint, the Daydream started to take on water. In an attempt to mend the issue, he brought in a 110-volt pump with a short in the wire to suction the water out. Mr. Williams plugged in the pump into an outlet while he and the wire were in the wading in the water. You can guess what happened: he died, right there. The craziest part about the whole thing was the dude *knew* about the faulty wire. I distinctly remember him telling me "Yeah, there's a short, but I know how to get this thing running." Famous last words. I could smell a lawsuit coming on, but nothing ever came of it.

***

When I got ready to go back to sea, the Marine Carrier put me on as Master on the Marine: my first Captain job, an honor I had been working toward for some time. It's said anything that's going to go wrong *will* go wrong on your first voyage as a captain – Murphy's Law and all that– and believe me, it's true. We loaded a cargo of grain and headed to Sicily, but I received a cable from the offices to skip Sicily and go to Crete if we had enough fuel. That put a big monkey on my back. I met with the chief engineer, Don Moore, and we figured if the ship burnt a barrel per mile, we could collect all the fuel into one tank and make it, safe and sound.

When we passed Sicily, headed for Crete, I admit I was nervous. Communication was a little slow. I finally received a message from my agent in Crete that Buckram Place had been hit by a storm. They informed me there was no fuel there, but that I could find some at the Northeast end of the island. My charts were very small scale and not for navigation purposes. I was afraid the fuel pumps would kick out because of the lowering pressure. But thankfully we made it, right around midnight.

I anchored the ship, and the fuel barge came along side to fill us up. What a relief that was. After fueling, we went from Crete to the Suez Canal and Egypt, through the Red Sea to the Indian Ocean and Karachi, Pakistan[5]. There we unloaded clean tanks and took on Number 6 fuel. Afterward, we made our way back to Portland, Oregon. Margaret and the kids picked me up in the car and we started the trip back to Kentucky.

What a trip it was. We went through these beautiful places – Seattle, Spokane, Yellowstone Park – and all the kids wanted to do was fight and complain. When we arrived in Kentucky, we loaded up our stuff and moved to Virginia. I was going to be Captain on the Commander for two years that was set to sail from Norfolk to Europe. It was a humdinger, to be sure, and I did that for a couple years, switching between two ships: the Commander and Producer, both of which were owned by Gino's dad.

*
**

As time moved along, Gino's dad sold off all but one of the Marine Carriers ships. The Producer was the only one left. I was the last remaining ship head, and therefore the only captain, in the entire company. I went home for a quick

---

[5] Right after we left, Egypt closed the Suez Canal until 1975, and 15 ships and their crew were trapped there for seven years.

vacation, and when the Producer came back to port I got ready to join her. But lo and behold, she had been sold, too. Her flags were being changed, but I was given the option to stay on as Chief Mate to break in the new Captain. I accepted. We set out for Karachi with 20,000 tons of ammonium nitrate. At that time, the U.S. and Pakistan were not the best of friends, and the folks in Pakistan refused to let us ship the cargo to Afghanistan. We stayed there for a couple of weeks, waiting in limbo before they moved us from Karachi to a port in Iran.

Word spread that they wanted us to ship the ammonium nitrate in trucks from Iran to Afghanistan. That plan never materialized, but we ended up staying in that grim location for about two weeks. It was *exceedingly* hot: 105 degrees every day and unbearably miserable. When we got back to Karachi, the flag was switched and a Spanish crew relieved us. I boarded a plane to San Francisco. Once we arrived, we were paid in cash, as was the law. Two guards with semi-automatic machine guns brought the money down. I took my earnings and caught a plane back to Nashville. The Marine Carriers didn't have any more ships, so there were no jobs for me. I just bided my time, waiting for another chance to go back to sea.

***

During my travels, I picked up authentic Ouzo, a popular alcoholic drink from Greece. My son, Tom, and his best friend, Harry Atkinson (who would later become Jackie's husband) always believed they could drink me under the table. So one time, when I was back in town on vacation, I took them up on the challenge. We started out on Scotch, because Tom, who was about 20 years old, fancied it a sophisticated drink. After we finished a bottle of that, we switched over to the Ouzo.

It didn't take long for old Tom to get right plastered. Before I knew it, he was stumbling around the house, loudly proclaiming his love for his girlfriend at the time, Margaret. You know, "Margaret this, Margaret that," that sort of thing. Keen to the hilarity of the situation, I broke out my tape recorder. It wasn't until after he finished his booze-drenched monologue that I showed him the tape recorder. He was in shock. I played the recording back to him, and man, the look on his face was priceless. He was so mad he threatened to *kill* me, though he eventually cooled down.

I think we drank every last drop of alcohol in the house that night, and Tom ended up hunched over the balcony, puking his guts out down onto the ground a story below.

***

After a while, I received a job offer from Keystone Shipping to be a Chief Mate on a tanker named the Cherry Valley. Keystone was a good company to work for, but I wasn't immediately awarded a Captain's position. I had to work my way up, prove myself all over again. They owned about 25 ships, and I did a lot of relieving as Captain. The permanent Captain would go on vacation and I would step in for a few months, then go back to being a Chief Mate upon his arrival. Keystone had three ships identical to the Cherry Valley, and one time, for about three months, I was a relief Captain on a chemical ship. That was an interesting job: there were about 50 different types of chemicals on board, and I had to make sure they stayed separated, because some of them (like paint thinners) were highly volatile. It was a touchy gig. We ran from Texas up the East Coast to Newhaven, Connecticut. That was the furthest we went.

The chemical ship was the first ship I was on that had a computer. I was technologically illiterate at the time, so one of the seamen gave me a crash course. The biggest thing I used it for was crew payroll. I had to put all the figures in the computer manually, and on one particular occasion suppertime rolled around while I was sending those paychecks out beautifully. I said "I'll run down and get me a bite to eat. No big deal." When I came back, that son of a buck had jammed up, and I had the biggest mess I've ever seen. I had to straighten the whole thing out, almost losing my religion right there: the same religion I found clinging to the railing underwater all those years earlier. It about drove me up a wall, but I made it through.

I stayed on the chemical ship until the full-time Captain came back, then took over a job as a permanent skipper on a tanker called the Cattaning. I joined it in the Persian Gulf, about 60 miles off the coast of Dubai, because the water wasn't deep enough for it to sail any closer. I flew into Dubai, and waited a couple of days for the ship to arrive. When it did, they put me on a tug boat and took me out to relieve the Captain.

I stayed on the Cattanning until the day I retired. We brought the ship back to Europe from the Persian Gulf. After we discharged the cargo, they put the ship on a charter with the Texaco Oil Company, which meant I was working for two bosses: Keystone for the crew and Texaco for the crude oil. For the next two years, I never knew exactly where we would be shipping out to next; it went trip-by-trip.

During my time on the Cattanning, I discovered that the North Sea is kind of like the Gulf of Mexico: there were a lot of oil rigs out there, and I was fine as long as I could see them, but a lot of the time it was very foggy. On the final trip of my seafaring career- from Scotland to the Bahamas - I learned there are more dangerous things to run into than a little fog.

10
Drunken Cooks and Rowdy Crews

"I went on a road trip with my cat, Cap'n. I would have let him drive, but he was drunk." - Jarod Kintz

Before recounting my tumultuous final journey at sea, I want to talk about one of the biggest headaches I had to deal with during my many years as a captain: the damn drunken cooks.

Our normal meal hours were 7:30-8:30 in the morning, 11:30-12:30 in the afternoon, and 5-6 in the evening. When the crew went down to the meal hall at those times, they expected the food to be ready. Most of the time, it wasn't. Something about cooking and drinking Jim Beam goes together, which explains why these cooks couldn't keep a job on shore for very long. Unfortunately, once we signed the drunkards to a ship, they were ours for six months. There was no way in hell the company was going to pay for their transportation back to the states.

Those cooks would buy armfuls of booze while we were at port, and if the Chief Mate, the Boson, or I found any, we tossed it over the side. We called it "sobering up the ship." When the cooks were particularly liquored up, they'd fight in the kitchen with knives and other utensils. The only place to lock them up was at the hospital, and they'd tear that to pieces, too.

I used to carry a pair of handcuffs with me. On the Producer, they had a fiddly in the engine room that blew hot air. That was my favorite spot for tying up the drunks. All I had to do was hook a drunkard up to a railing near a fiddly and it sobered him up right away. The steam took its toll. On one occasion, this particular cook got so toasted he couldn't even stand up, so I hooked him to the top rail. He was lying on the ground at an awkward angle, arm cocked uncomfortably overhead. When we got back to the states, he brought a suit against me and the company, claiming he had come down with arthritis. It was eventually settled out of court, saving everybody involved a big headache. There was never a dull moment, that's for sure.

On one trip, I had to get rough with a few guys to bring them to their senses. I knew they would eventually try to get even with me, so I quit eating anything that came out of the galley. I lived for about three months on nothing but those small individual boxes of cereal, and I even looked those over to make sure they hadn't been tampered with.

***

One time, we had a load of grain bound for Manila in the Philippines, and my good friend Gino had a ship full of cargo going in Subic Bay that was destined for Vietnam. There had been some sort of mix-up, causing the ship to be docked for an abnormally long period of time. The crew was refused shore leave, so in a fit of what you might call "cabin fever," the seamen ended up having a violent free-for-all. Gino asked if I wanted to ride up there with him to straighten everything out. I said "Sure, why not?"

We took the same route that the Japanese took in WWII when they captured American and Filipino prisoners of war and forced them to march to Camp O'Donnell. The "Bataan Death March," is what they call it. There were signs along the side of the road that displayed how many people died at each particular section of the path. The march started in Mariveles, Bataan and ended at the prison camp in San Fernando, Pampanga, but thousands of people died before reaching the destination. The Japanese Army was charged with a war crime for it. U.S. Congressional Representative Dana Rohrbacher described the Death March in terse, brutal language while paying homage to the victims in 2001:

They were beaten, and they were starved as they marched. Those who fell were bayoneted. Some of those who fell were beheaded by Japanese officers who were practicing with their samurai swords from horseback. The Japanese culture at that time reflected the view that any warrior who surrendered had no honor; thus was not to be treated like a human being. Thus they were not committing crimes against human being...the Japanese soldiers at that time...felt they were dealing with subhumans and animals.

When we arrived in Subic Bay, it was like *we* were dealing with subhumans and animals. It was a drunken free-for-all. The crew was out of control, chasing one another with axes. Gino calmed them down, and eventually the ship was moved to Vietnam. When I got back to the United States, I went home to Virginia. I was only there a few days when I got a call from the office asking if I would be interested in paying off that ship. It had ported at Norfolk, and as soon as it landed the captain – completely distraught – took off, shunning the payroll and everything.

I've never seen such a mess of paperwork in my life. There were no records. The ship had been gone at sea for nine months and the crew was owed overtime. A couple of other guys and I eventually got everything straightened out. The final tally was $100,000. The money was brought down from the banks in bags, and it would have taken forever to count it all, so we simply checked to see if the seals were intact and signed for it. After that, I dispensed the money to each individual crew member.

I made my way through that mess, and I'm all beaten down and tired, and all of sudden I find out I'm $1,000 short. Talk about your stomach dropping: the last thing I wanted to do was cover the difference on my own dime. I spoke with an agent, and it turned out the bank shorted me one grand. The crisis was pacified. It felt like a weight was lifted off my shoulders.

11
George's Final Voyage – Battling Hurricane Josephine

"Despite my pain, I felt not the regret of an ending, but the foreboding of a beginning." - Robin Hobb

We finished our contract in the North Sea and sailed for Hounds Point, Scotland to load cargo. We were loading close to 80,000 barrels per hour and inadvertently let one of the tanks get too full. The next thing I knew, there was foam spewing onto the mast and oil was raining on the deck. I got on the radio and told the dock "Shut it down! You're spewing oil!" Thankfully, we nipped the crisis in the bud before it became a full-on catastrophe. That was the closest I ever came to a spill. It's not something I'd want to experience again.

In retrospect, the near spill seems like a grim omen for the heightened trouble I would experience soon thereafter. We set sail for the Bahamas, taking the Great Circle out of Scotland. Texaco ordered us to run at "economy speed" (10 knots) to preserve fuel. We were chugging along when I received a radio report saying hurricane Josephine was working its way Northwest through the Bahamas. I assured myself that it would be long gone before we got there, but that stubborn son of a gun set up shop just north of the Bahamas.

We kept plugging along, and every day we drew a little closer to the storm. I kept waiting for the thing to move, but it wasn't going anywhere. It was a serious and powerful hurricane, winds around 150 miles an hour or so. We began to feel the breeze 300 miles north of it, and I said "Man, I have to do something about this."

I pulled out my Bowditch – the seaman's bible, as it were – to make sure I was approaching this hurricane in the right manner. It instructed me to put the wind on the port quarter and go like hell. I contacted Keystone and Texaco and Amber[6] to let them know I was changing course and speed because of an emergency. I told them any expenses incurred would be split up between everyone involved.

After I got the go-ahead, I cranked it up to 17 knots. We encountered heavy wind and big waves. Thankfully, only one wave – this giant mountain of water – came aboard, but it didn't do any damage because we were sailing full speed away from it. I was afraid the hurricane would move toward the west and we would run directly into it. That didn't happen, but we met very high winds for a sustained amount of time. The anemometer on the mast of the ship (which keeps track of wind speed) broke off when the wind reached 90 mph.

Inside the wheel house, I could feel the bulkheads breathing as the gusts of wind ripped through. The visibility was nil. We were experiencing heavy rain, and the hurricane winds were picking off the tops of the waves and throwing the water on board. We had two radars, but all I could see for three miles was sea return.

---

[6] The United States' way of keeping track of ships at sea.

Around midnight, when the wind was at top speed, we got a call on the radio saying there was an airplane circling the area, searching for a sailboat. He wanted to know if we had seen it. I told him all we could see was water. Later on, I learned a sailboat sank in the tempest.

***

We finally made our way past Josephine, somehow still in one piece. Right after we left Scotland, I got a telex that said our deck officers[7] would be relieved by a non-union crew when we arrived at Port Arthur. That meant our job was finished. I had been considering retirement, and the news of the replacement crew sealed the deal for me. I sent a telex saying I was going to call it a career when I reached shore.

The first person that came aboard after the ship was cleared by the health and immigration commission was the Captain set to relieve me. I spoke with a representative from the company office, and he offered me an opportunity to stay on as a Captain in a non-union role. He said he would equal my retirement package and pay from the union. The only catch was they didn't have an age limit, so to get 20 years on the job I would have had to sail until I was about 80 years old. That didn't sound appealing to me, so I rejected the offer.

I handed the ship over to the other Captain, and the deck officers and I went ashore in groups, escorted by Federal Marshals. Apparently, the Feds were afraid we were going to sabotage the ship. If they escorted us off the deck, the

---

[7] The Captain, Chief Mate, Second Mate and Third Mate.

thinking went, we couldn't face accusations if anything shady went down. When we reached the gate, I said "Adios!"

That was a hell of a way to leave my last ship. As a proud Captain, it didn't sit well with me, but there wasn't much I could do. I hitched a ride in a cab and went to the motel to call Margaret. I told her to pick me up at St. Petersburg Airport. From there, I went to the union hall in Norfolk to sign my retirement papers.

Just like that, my seagoing career was over. It was October 1984. I was 62 years old. I probably could have kept going for another couple of years, but it would have been tough. It was strange to think it was all over – the open sea, the battles with formidable tempests, even the damn drunken cooks – but as I've realized many times throughout my life, all good things must come to an end. With the sea behind me, I once again returned to land, this time for good, to pursue leisurely activities and spend some with my family.

12
Margaret's Trips

"A man with a good wife is the luckiest of God's creatures..."
- Stephen King

Margaret always enjoyed the open sea, and throughout our 50-plus years together we sailed to a lot of beautiful locations. We loved the water so much that after our kids moved away from home, we sold our house and lived on a boat for three years. We lived a year in Virginia on the Chickahominy River, then we moved the boat down to St. Petersburg for two years. Margaret had always wanted to experience the deep sea with me while I was a Captain, but we had three kids that needed to be cared for. Eventually, we made a deal with a woman who agreed to stay at the house and look after them while we were on the water.

Most companies don't allow any crew members - even officers - to bring their wives on a trip, but Marine Carriers wasn't too strict in that regard. They were fine with it. Margaret went to the Coast Guard office to file papers to become the ship's librarian. Whenever we signed a document, I was George, the Captain, and she was Margaret, the librarian.

On Margaret's maiden voyage, we departed from Baltimore. We set sail for India, taking off through the Atlantic and over to the Gibraltar Straights. She had never seen anything like that before, and she was absolutely enthralled. We stopped for fuel in August, Sicily, and had to wait our turn to head through the canal. That night, during some down time, we went to an upscale restaurant and had an incredible seafood dinner. Afterward, we tossed our scraps on the floor for dogs to polish off. It sounds strange, but that's just the way things are done in Augusta.

We came back to the ship the next morning and it was our turn to go through the canal. The Egyptian pilot that led us through kept gazing at Margaret's body as she sunbathed on the deck. It roiled me, but I let it slide. This particular trip we could see all of these beautiful, picturesque islands as we passed through the canal. We ended up in the port city of Kandla, which is in the Northern part of India, near Bombay. The first port on the Indian Ocean between Pakistan and India is Bombay, so Kerala was built so ships wouldn't have to travel as far.

Kerala is fairly large port, but that's literally all it was: there was no city there, very little civilization. Margaret, a devout Southern Baptist, was interested in finding a nearby church. Whenever the agent from the company came on board, she asked him to direct her to the closest place of worship. He told her the nearest city was 12 miles away, and that it had a movie theatre and a church, too. This agent was delightfully cooperative, and arranged for us to attend a service there.

On Sunday morning, he sent a car to pick us up. On our way to the service, we saw camel carts and all kinds of indigenous traffic. Very few cars, though. When we got to the church, we were led to the second floor. Inside, 30-40 people were sitting on the ground. Women were on one side of the aisle, men were on the other. The pastor knew we were coming, so there were two chairs in the back of the room waiting for us.

The pastor spoke in the native language. We were the only English speakers in the congregation, so there was an interpreter present. He imitated all of the pastor's movements and kept up, word-for-word. I'd give anything to have a video of it. It was wild. The preacher went on for about an hour and the interpreter was still going strong, but there was a prearranged time for us to leave. After some time had passed, an agent came up to us and said "Let's go." I gave them a nice donation before I left, which, I think, was the main thing they were looking for. Margaret talked about that sermon until the day she died.

***

A few years later, Margaret joined me on a trip to Holland. We distributed our kids to some of our relatives, although this time it was much harder to find someone to watch after them. People don't mind taking care of young kids, but once they start growing up nobody wants to look after them. Imagine that.

It was a relatively short trip, about a month long, there and back. Margaret swooned over Amsterdam, she thought it was a great city with interesting people. At docks in America, you always see scrap metal and old machinery lying around. It wasn't like that in Amsterdam; everything was very clean, and there were beautiful tulips growing over there, gorgeous fields brimming with flowers all in bloom. It made for a surreal picture. When we weren't marveling at the scenery, we visited museums and restaurants and did a lot of sightseeing. Margaret really enjoyed that, it was one of the things she remembered most about our life together.

Coming back from Amsterdam, we encountered a storm. On most ships, there are sturdy, built-in beds to minimize the chance of them rocking around during rough weather. But on the Producer, someone replaced those sturdy beds with regular beds, which still had hooks to hold them in place. I was up on the bridge, and all of a sudden I heard yelling down below. I went to see what was going on, and the BR (the guy that cleans the room and makes the bed) had removed the bed from the hooks so he could clean. There was Margaret, screaming bloody murder, sliding back and forth across the floor on the mattress like an egg in a frying pan. She couldn't get off it. I eventually saved her and put the bed back on the hooks. We laughed about that for years.

Part Three

13
George Ashore (Permanently)

"Life is a series of natural and spontaneous changes. Don't resist them; that only creates sorrow. Let reality be reality. Let things flow naturally forward in whatever way they like."
- Lao Tzu

Margaret and I owned a motor home, so immediately after I retired we decided to do some traveling. While we were visiting my parents in Kentucky, we discovered a 33-acre farm for sale. I said "Man, that might be a good place to have if the union goes sour on my pension. I could always eat potatoes on the farm, just like the old days." We decided to buy it, and ended up living there for about 10 years. It was one of the best decades of my life.

In 1988, it was finally announced that Merchant Marines who served during World War II – specifically from Dec. 7, 1941 to Aug. 15 1945 – were to receive veterans status, a ruling that I had been anxiously awaiting. We had experienced wartime conditions, after all. Our lives had been at risk. One out of 26 Merchant Marines who served during World War II didn't make it out alive. Why *shouldn't* we be recognized alongside the official branches of the military? And to think, a year or so after I joined the Merchant Marines, a military recruiter from Hopkinsville was calling me a draft dodger and attempting to force me to join a branch of the armed forces.

Anyway, around the time I received veteran status, my old buddy, Jack Marshall, got me started in the cattle business and I bought a John Deere tractor. I loved that tractor, especially considering I grew up on a farm where all we owned was a plow and a mule. It reminded me of Jim Williamson's tractor.

During my decade on that farm, my mother passed away. She was 88 years old. My pop was still living on the place on 19th street I helped buy all those years ago. After mom passed, he didn't want to live there anymore: he was alone, his hearing was going downhill, and a lot of coloreds had moved to the area. We sold the place and decided to buy him a single wide trailer with two bedrooms and move him out to our farm. We put a deck on the front of it, so him and Rosie – that was my dog – could sit out there and watch me work.

It was around this time that I fully accepted Jesus Christ as my lord and savior. I did it one Sunday morning at Rocky Ridge Baptist Church in Trigg County, Kentucky. Though I've considered myself a Christian for most of my life, this was the moment I truly began to take my eternal fate seriously. I still consider it one of the most important days of my existence. It has given me much peace of mind over the past 24 years, as I move closer and closer to the Great Beyond.

After a decade on the farm, a real estate agent asked if I was interested in selling the place. I told her "Sure, if the price is right." She said "What kind of price are you looking at?" I jacked that thing up quite a bit and said "I'll take that." I sold pop's trailer along with it and gave him the money.

I wasn't quite sure what to do next. Margaret wanted to go back to Virginia because she was originally from Richmond and a lot of our grandkids lived there. Eventually, that's what we did. We packed up our stuff, had an auctioneer sell off everything we didn't want, and put the rest in a U-Haul. We found a place in Powhatan, Virginia with 10 acres and a three bedroom house. We had it all figured out.

***

Vicky helped us move. At the time, we had a pontoon boat. We hauled it behind the truck and hooked the trailer – which had the bush hog and the tractor in it – behind the U-Haul. Vicky followed me to Virginia. Tom was riding with me and Margaret was riding with Vicky. Jackie was in North Carolina with her husband, Harry Atkinson, who also happened to be Tom's best friend.

The first night on the road we waited too long and couldn't find a hotel. We were near an airport, so I knew there had to be hotels *somewhere* in the area. We pulled onto a road that made a circle around the airport. There I am pulling this farm tractor behind a U-Haul, and Vicky's right on my tail pulling a pontoon boat. We must have been quite a sight. I'm sure we looked like country bumpkins.

After driving around for a while we finally found a motel. We decided to get supper, and before we left I unhitched the pontoon boat from the truck. When I tried to hook it back up after supper, I must not have gotten the ball fully on the hitch because the next morning, after we pulled onto the road, I got a call on my CB radio from Vicky saying "Dad! Dad! The trailer's coming loose!" I pulled over to the shoulder and sure enough the pontoon boat had come off the ball, but thankfully the chain held it in place. I hooked it back up and we made our way toward Powhatan.

The place needed some maintenance and upkeep, but the house was only about five years old and in great condition. When I first looked into buying it, I got a call from the owner saying the stable had burnt down: the guy had mowed his lawn and put the mower back in hot, torching the building. I told him we'd make a deal, but I wasn't going to pay for a stable that didn't exist. We ended up getting enough money knocked off the price to pay for a stable later on.

I had always wanted to build something, and that stable was my experiment. It had three stalls, an open room for storing feed, and a loft for keeping bales of hay. It was a community project: Vicky and Jack helped, but Tom wasn't involved. He was down in Florida slicing corn beef at his restaurant, Corn Beef Corner. Pop witnessed the building of the stable: he watched us work from his chair in the shade, Rosie by his side.

After we got the place looking nice, I gave Jackie, Vicky and Tom an acre a-piece, just in case they wanted to build a house there. I had this grand idea of starting a familial community where all my children would own a house. Vicky eventually put a doublewide on her lot. She was working for Capital One at the time, but ended up transferring to Florida.

***

Margaret and I bought a vacation place at Fisherman's Cove in Tavares, Florida. It was a campground, more or less, that had an RV set-up station right on sight complete with a car port, a utility room, and a screen room. We spent about six months out of the year there and had someone else look after the place in Powhatan. We were regular snowbirds.

I enjoyed Tavares immensely. I took my pontoon boat down there and fished for crappie at night. The place had a nine-hole golf course, and every Friday the community hosted a tournament: The men and women would draw names to determine partners, and there was a cash payout for first, second, and third place. I ended up getting pretty good at golf.

In the meantime, Jackie ran into some misfortune. She and Harry were in the restaurant business. They had a couple places doing well, but they bought one in Midlothian called Coalfields that didn't do so hot. I told her she could move into the house in Powhatan and look after it. I thought it was going to be a temporary arrangement, but that's not how it turned out. Jackie's still there now, and she's taking good care of the place.

After we came back from Florida, I hauled my Fifth Wheel around and did a lot of traveling. I built a deck that I could back the trailer up to. We did that for a couple of years. But then Margaret's health started going downhill. It happened incrementally, consistently. We went to Vicky's place in Powhatan that we had bought from her because of the job transfer, and that's where Margaret met her maker. Her health had been going south for a long time, and we had been spending many hours at doctors and hospitals and finally it got to the point where she was turned over to hospice. It was a very sad time; we were married for over 50 years and had a great life together. When we buried her in Powhatan, we bought a matching grave for me.

After Margaret's death, Vicky took great care of me, changing her way of life just to help out. Margaret was a good mother to her, and I suppose that was Vicky's way of paying homage. I really appreciate all she did. Of course, Jackie and Tom were always there for us, too.

After Margaret's death, I found out how lonely life can be after losing your partner prematurely.

14
Losses and Gains

"Don't grieve. Anything you lose comes round in another form."- Rumi

When Margaret passed, I really didn't have much to do. Losing your partner of 52 years is a lonesome life. You feel like a knot on a log, you don't blend in any more. I ended up back in Tavares, where I passed a particularly painful kidney stone, to add insult to what I was already going through. I've had kidney stones about every three years all of my adult life, but this one sticks out as particularly painful. I was getting ready to go to Florida, so Tom and I got together to drink a little Jim Beam. I left Tom's place, and when I arrived in Tavares I discovered I had a urinary tract infection.

For about two weeks, all I did was lie on the couch. My next door neighbors - really nice people - took care of me. One of my neighbors said "I thought you were going to die!" I said "I thought I was too, to tell you the truth." I was so sick I suffered from hallucinations, and during one of them I saw a pretty woman on TV advertising the purple pill. I said "Damn, that looks like Martha Bush!" So I decided to go back to Hopkinsville to find her.

I had known Martha for a long time. She had spent some time as a waitress at the Rock Café, and was good friends with Margaret for many years. When I was about 25 years old, someone introduced me to her while I was home on vacation. I asked her on a date, but she said she had other plans. Her refusal turned out to be a blessing in disguise, because although she had been telling everybody she was 18, she was really only 16. I didn't think much about Martha after that, didn't ask her on a second date until *many* years later.

Margaret had passed away in August, and I headed to Hopkinsville around Christmas. Martha's late husband, Frank, who I used to play golf with, had died about eight years prior. She had never remarried. I asked her out to dinner, and afterward we went back to the hotel I was staying at. We talked for hours and hours. That was the beginning of George and Martha.

After our night together, I returned to Powhatan. We talked on the phone every evening like young lovers. Our telephone romance lasted quite a while and things were beginning to blossom, so I decided to go back to Hopkinsville to propose to her. Lo and behold, Martha said yes.

On the one hand, I thought I may be rushing things, considering it had only been five months since Margaret's death. But I had to put things behind me. It was the only way to move on.

***

On January 29, 2004, Martha and I asked a preacher at Rocky Ridge Church in Trigg County to marry us. We fixed up a ceremony at the church, and I walked up the aisle and said "I do." One of my good friends, John Hancock, was dating one of Martha's friends. John ended up being my best man and his girlfriend was Martha's maid of honor. Martha and I decided to go to Tavares for our honeymoon. She liked it down there, just like Margaret did. I had sold my Fifth Wheel and my pontoon boat when Margaret was sick because we weren't traveling very often. Naturally, I had to get another pontoon boat. There's a big lake between Tavares and Leesburg called Lake Harris that runs all the way up to Sage Islands River and down to Jacksonville. The water was virtually unlimited. We spent winters in Tavares and traveled up to Powhatan during summers.

Eventually, Martha and I decided to get a permanent place in Hopkinsville. We found a two acre spot on 2002 Lover's Lane. I made a written deal with Jackie saying she could take over the farm and the house in Virginia. Jackie was still working at the County Seat restaurant in Powhatan, and her two kids - Matt and Jake - took good care of the place. Jackie's husband, Harry, was still living, but he had a bad accident on a horse that severely damaged his internal organs. The horse threw him against a tree and then came down on top of him. I'm not sure he ever recovered, to tell you the truth. A few years later he came down with pancreatic cancer and not too much later he was gone. It was a tough time because Harry had been close with everyone in our family.

I stayed busy at my new place on Lover's Lane, cleaning up, cutting down trees, and other general maintenance. I got it so the entire two acres could be mowed without stopping. I decided to sell my place in Tavares because I caught wind of a guy who was coming into the area to build condos. I said

"I'm going to get out of here before I'm forced to move and don't get a cent." It was a sad day when we left Fisherman's Cove. I really loved that place – the golf, the unlimited water, everything. But all things have to come to an end, even the good things. I brought my pontoon boat back to Kentucky.

***

Martha and I were down in Florida visiting Vicky, and at about two in the morning my phone rang. It was Martha's youngest daughter, calling to say the Lover's Lane house was on fire. That's a hell of a way to be woken up. I don't recommend it.

By three o'clock we were in the motor home heading north, and when we reached the house the following day it was completely torched. It was a brick house, so some of the walls were still standing, but all the internal parts were gone. The inclined driveway was so iced over I couldn't drive the motor home up there. Thankfully, our next door neighbors had an apartment over their garage that they let us stay in for a couple of days.

Though the official cause of the fire was never determined, the fire marshal hypothesized that a mouse was the culprit. The way he explained made sense: mice will often seek refuge in attics during the winter months, but once they get up there, they find the food supply virtually non-existent. In what I guess could be called an act of desperation, these mice start gnawing on anything they can find – including the insulation around electrical lines. This can create sparks, and sparks can lead to fire, and fire can lead to...well, you get the idea. It's a crazy world, I tell you. You never know what's going to happen next.

When the insurance adjuster came out, the first thing he did was give me $5,000 for incidental expenses. He also said the insurance company would pay the rent on wherever we ended up staying. There was a hunting lodge right across the street from Lover's Lane. We checked it out, and lo and behold the owner was the daughter of a friend I knew back in the day. We stayed there for six months.

***

In January, not too long after the house burnt down, my preacher and his wife invited Martha and I to dinner. We went to a steakhouse in Fort Campbell, and as I was walking out of the restaurant after the meal, I slipped on an ice-covered stepping stone and landed hard on my right hip. They called an ambulance and wanted to take me to a hospital in Fort Bell. I'm allergic to anything with the word "Fort" in the name – I had bad experiences with the Army, Navy and Coast Guard in the past – so I didn't want anything to do with those people. I said "Nah, I'm not going," and decided to walk it off. On the way back to Hopkinsville, the pain started to become unbearable. I told them to take me to the emergency room. That's when it was confirmed I had broken my leg two inches below the hip bone. A clean break. They didn't have any surgeons at this particular hospital, so they sent me to a bigger one in Nashville. They fixed me up and said "You are going to be all right," and I said "Good."

I spent quite a few days in the hospital before going back to Hopkinsville. I was on crutches and in a wheel chair, so Martha had to take care of me like an old mother hen. Talk about your luck going south. The house burning down, the broken leg...I was in a very hard spot at that time. Eventually I healed up. I haven't had many problems with my leg recently – no limping or anything like that.

*
**

In March, we got a contract to rebuild the house. We found a builder that had erected a house for one of Martha's friends. We loved it so much we patterned our house after it. I had a contract for moving the debris from the burnt house, and the builder told me I could save big money by digging a hole on the backside – I call it my "Back 40" – and tossing the debris in there. He dug a hole about 30-feet wide and 30-feet deep, using all kinds of equipment. It was pouring down rain the day he was going to move the debris into the hole, and he was using a dump truck, so he would have torn up the Back 40 if he tried to drive on it. As an alternative, he took the debris to a place on Crested Road.

The hole was still back there, of course, so we had to figure out a use for it. As the house was being rebuilt, we threw some of the excess scraps in the hole, along with an old stable my neighbor, Bob, gutted out. We had a heck of a fire – a christening, of sorts, for the new place. We eventually leveled it off. It has sunken down over the years, but it's not much of a bother. I seeded the Back 40, and got the grass looking nice.

By July 1, the place was move-in ready. The insurance paid for us to refurnish and restock the house, so Martha had a ball of a shopping spree. Everything was coming together once again, and as I approached my 90th birthday, I awaited the arrival of my friends and family for a celebration of my nine decades on Earth.

15
Bringing it All Back Home

"You must remember, family is often born of blood, but it doesn't depend on blood. Nor is it exclusive of friendship. Family members can be your best friends, you know. And best friends, whether or not they are related to you, can be your family."- Trenton Lee Stewart

By late August, we were settled into our new place. It's nice, we're happy. All of my kids (Tom, Vicky, Jackie) and Martha's kids (Allison, Rhonda and Vicky Lee) are still living. Allison, Rhonda and Vicky Lee are like my kids now – we get along very well. We're getting ready for a big year. I still sail with Jack Marshall every once and a while. He's two years older than I am and hanging in there. He's been a great friend to me all my life.

As I've mentioned, Jack and I became like brothers – probably closer than brothers. Jack is as good a friend and person as I've ever met. Though he doesn't have much formal education, he has a strong mind and a lot of "know how." He's a farm boy, born and raised. When his dad passed away, Mr. Marshall divided up the farm out in New Bethlehem between Jack and his two siblings. The industrial park in Clarksville wanted to buy the farm, and Jack's oldest son – a lawyer – negotiated and ended up getting $1.2 million for the place. Even though Jack isn't what you'd call a "money person," that made him very happy.

Martha and I still visit him every so often. When we go over there, Martha and Jack's wife, Charlotte, will go in one room and Jack and I will sit in another part of the house and reminisce. It's always a pleasure talking about the good old days. Jack is looking old, but I guess I'm looking pretty old myself.

So what is there left to say? I've had a good life. Sometimes it was pretty tricky, but all-in-all I had good people around me. Next Friday is May 2, 2014, and I will be 90 years old. Can you imagine living 90 years in this world? Whoa, it's been rough. All my kids are coming to visit for my birthday, and Tom is bringing his two daughters, Caitlin and Meghan. Jackie's kids, Jake and Matt, won't be making the trip. Matt just landed a good job in Washington, D.C., working for a marketing company that promotes Republican candidates, even though he's not a Republican. He's got an MBA, smart as a tack. Jake has been the head cook at Jackie's restaurant for a while now. He's going to look after the place while Jackie is visiting. Jack and Charlotte are making the trip from Clarksville. We're going to have quite a crowd here. It'll be nice to be surrounded by good people.

It's sad to say, but I don't know how much longer I'm going to last. I don't have the energy I once had. I still mow my yard, keep it cleaned up. I've got some flowers out there and a place out back to keep my RV that we take to the lake every so often. I still take out the old pontoon boat for a spin every once and a while. I also have a fishing boat and a canoe. I have all these toys but I don't have the energy to use them anymore. I guess I'll just bide my time. Who knows what will happen down the road? I might break 100 one day. Why not? I'd welcome it.

***

I think this is the end of my book. Looks like I'm finishing on my birthday. It's almost as hard to wrap us as it was to start. It has been quite a humdinger trying to get all these thoughts on a recorder. I hope I don't push a button and delete the whole thing. That would be rough, wouldn't it? I'd never be able to repeat everything.

Anyway, what else is there to say? It's been a good one. I'm going to say "Sayonara." I don't know what that means, but everybody says that.

This is what you call the end. Adios. Goodbye.

Afterword

February 11, 2015
12:02 a.m.

It was late January 2015, when Tom, Caitlin, and I piled into Tom's truck and set out for Hopkinsville, Kentucky. It's about an eight hour drive from Tom's house in Botetourt, Virginia, to George's place on 2002 Lover's Lane, and for the first few hours it was all mountains and hillsides, but not long after we crossed into Tennessee, barreling ever-closer to the Midwest, the landscape flattened out like the face of a nickel. When we finally pulled into George' driveway, a neighbor's Australian Shepherd with one brown eye and one blue eye greeted us with love and a dangling tongue.

"If you really want to get some good material, just hang around him for a while," said George's wife, Martha, a few hours after we arrived. "I'll be in here watching television and all of a sudden he'll start up on one of his sea stories. Before I know it, the volume's turned all the way down and I'm sitting there listening to him talk about the good old days."

It didn't take long for me to discover the truth of that statement. Fortunately, the television was turned off for much of the weekend – except when we watched the Seahawks literally throw away the Super Bowl and an engrossing special on Nazi Hunters – so George had plenty of time to sift through his tightly-packed memory for thoughts and stories from yesteryear. There was that time a man electrocuted himself to death while working on George's personal boat, the Daydream, while George was out at sea. And the time Tom thought he could drink George under the table, only to get plastered on scotch and Grecian Ouzo. Not to mention the endless well of tales from the open sea. The stories unfurled naturally (aided by Tom's contributions) and I kept the recorder app on my IPhone at the ready (as did Caitlin), preparing for the next moment George would dust off some pristine diamond from his past. I came home that Monday with over three hours worth of George' s stories, the majority of which I was able to use in the body of this book.

George, though only four months away from his 91st birthday, somehow seemed in better shape – mentally, physically, spiritually – than the rest of us. He cracked jokes quicker than I could process them, and told stories with more depth and detail than I ever considered possible for a near-centenarian. He is also a graceful drinker (and a fan of Busch Light), which is perhaps unsurprising, considering he is both an accomplished captain *and* a Southern Gentleman – two check marks in the right column when it comes to being an efficient consumer of alcohol.

Perhaps most importantly, his eyes were still lively. That's something Tom emphasized the importance of: the vitality of those *eyes*. And it's true. Eyes tend to relay information directly from the soul, and in George's case, the message read "Everything is fine behind the scenes." And speaking of scenes, on the Saturday of our visit, George decided to take the four of us – Martha, Tom, Caitlin, and I – on a pick-up truck tour of the settings that played major roles in his youth. Schools, churches, houses, athletic fields – if it was pertinent to George's childhood, we most likely drove by it.

Now, while George's current residence is located in a generally suburban area, it's a short drive in any direction to vast fields of hemp and corn and various other crops. It's an extreme type of rural-ness, one that elicits a feeling of timelessness that settles heavily in the gut, and as you look out across those green fields stretching out for miles to meet the horizon it all seems mystical and ancient. The 21st century has yet to fully permeate this part of the country, and while there are plenty of modern amenities and contemporary surroundings near George's current homestead, this part of the country is like stepping back in time a full century. *This* is the Kentucky George grew up in. Several times we drove by kids riding old style bicycles, wearing old style clothes, looking as though they'd never even heard of the internet. Not much has changed around here, it seems. And that only adds to its antiquated mystique.

We hit all the main landmarks from George's childhood: his birthplace, the Old West House (which is now in a certain state of disrepair); the little yellow house on 19th street George helped purchase for his parents; the old Hopkinsville High School football field, complete with stone bleachers; Ralston School, where George used to play baseball and fetch watermelons from the stream; the old dirt road that split his parent's families' farms (Albert's family's on the left, Pansy's family's on the right). We also stopped at landmarks not directly related to George's heritage, like the Jefferson Davis Memorial in Fairview, which can best be described as the Washington Monument en miniature, shooting up out of the endless flatness like some sort of Gray Confederate Mecca. We also climbed to the top of Pilot Rock, which, in spite of the unsightly graffiti, offered a breathtaking panoramic view of the Kentucky countryside. Our final stop was a local BBQ joint. Tom bought a rack of ribs for half price because the place was preparing to close for the evening.

"Got dang, can't beat that deal," Tom hollered as we climbed back into the truck.

On the morning of our departure back to Virginia, George beat Caitlin and me out of bed, just like he had the entire time we were there. He loaded us up with extra food for the trip, and then we said our goodbyes. George is a good man with an addictive sense of humor, and I think all of us were a little forlorn that the trip was coming to an end. He and Martha had been outstanding hosts. A few days earlier I was in George's office, surrounded by books and memorabilia from his seafaring days, watching him lean back in his swivel chair while recounting the most vivid memories of his 90-plus years on Earth. That moment is something I will always cherish. Learning about his story has been a perspective-altering experience, one that has taught me, among other things, what it means to be a man, and how to extract the most meaning out of our painfully short time on this Earth.

As we packed the truck, the Australian Shepherd was nowhere to be found. After a round of hugs, we took off across the flatness, the early morning gray slowly progressing into daylight as we passed the famous Nashville skyline, the Sunsphere in Knoxville, and other sights that we knew we may not see again for quite some time. We listened, mostly, to Lost on the River: The New Basement Tapes, a collection of songs written by Marcus Mumford, Elvis Costello, and others based on old Bob Dylan lyrics that recently had been discovered, and never used.

Eventually, the flatness disappeared, and in its place mountains sprouted. As we entered Virginia, the snow fell heavily. But by the time we reached Botetourt, the sun had broken through the clouds, and everything seemed right and safe again.

"That was a good weekend," Caitlin said a little while later. "I'm glad we went."

We all agreed, silently but fully.

From the top of Pilot Rock

Made in the USA
Middletown, DE
07 May 2015